What Are You Waiting For?
(So Act Already!)

The Unsociable Business of Social
Networks
&
Why the So Act Social Network Will
Change the World

What Are You Waiting For?
(So Act Already!)

The Unsociable Business of Social Networks
&
Why the So Act Social Network Will Change the World

By

Jon W. Hansen

Foreword

S o Act wasn't created to build a better network, it was created to build a better world."

After announcing that I would be writing a book contemplating the emerging significance and probable impact of So Act in the evolving Social Media hierarchy, the above line was the lead quote attributed to me in the Network's October 27th press release.

While this may lead some to conclude that I am a paid for hire wordsmith whose colorful prose is more reflective of a healthy financial arrangement rather than objective journalism, nothing could be further from the truth.

Do not get me wrong, I am being paid (in fact in advance) by So Act to write this book. But at this stage in my career and life I have learnt that financial gain no matter how rewarding, is much like fame in that it is ephemeral in nature. As a one-time multi-millionaire who once graced the mansions of Ambassadors and shared the spotlight with Kuwaiti Sheiks, it all counts for naught at the end of one's days.

What does last, and in the spirit of the Albert Pike quote (although some have attributed it to Abraham Lincoln) "What we have done for ourselves alone dies with us; what we have done for others and the world remains and is immortal," is the sustaining value of one's contribution to society as a whole. This belief is probably why the So Act story caught my attention in the first place. It is also the reason why the flame of passion that is so necessary to write was fanned within me.

In short, if I did not believe in the premise or principles of So Act, I could have been offered all the money in the world and would not have been able to write a word. Well, maybe a word or even possibly a sentence or two, but certainly not a work that I would feel good about, nor one you would want to read. Take my word for it when I say this, the So Act story is a book you will want to read and share.

So Act is the 60 Minutes of social networks . . . probing, assertive, informed and balanced. So Act is not just another social network, but is a venue that engages, informs, cross-pollinates and mobilizes.

As social media veterans and thought leaders have noted, the impact of emerging platforms such as the Twitters and Facebooks extends well beyond the ability to simply connect, take dating quizzes and exchange information about favourite movies or what someone had for dinner. There is a growing realization that social networks can be an instrument to make valuable contributions that translate into sustainable change. Clearly there is a need to engage and mobilize champions of change into a collaborative and collective force for positive action through dynamic and well informed conversational ex-changes.

Recognizing these immutable truths, and using the social media world as a point of reference, this book will focus on the timeliness and influential nature of So Act's unique platform.

We will touch on key building areas including the Network's ability to create sustainable traction through the combination of next generation technology and a commitment to be a positive force for change in the increasingly complex world that is the global community.

At the end of this text I will hopefully have provided you with a balanced view of what may very well become the model against which all other social networks and revenue models will be measured.

In the call to action words of So Act founder and visionary Greg Halpern . . . "What are you waiting for - So Act Already," and enjoy the book!

Table of Contents

Chapter 1 - Dissention Sows the Seeds of Optimism

". . . the combination of organizational dissatisfaction, vision for the future and the possibility of immediate, tactical action must be stronger than the resistance within the organization in order for meaningful changes to occur."

Gleicher's Formula for Change

W hen I first undertook this journey to better understand the aligned realms of the emerging world of social networking and social media, with the conscientious elements of that which appeals to our better angels or nature, the task intrigued me on a number of levels.

To begin, assigning both the individual and collective roles each play in successfully balancing technological capitalism while simultaneously stimulating social change would suggest an uneasy alliance. While the former may conjure up images from Joseph Conrad's Heart of Darkness, which extends the battle between good and evil to one of humanity's struggle with its own morals, the latter suggests a view that is more in line with the Alcestis of Euripides. Specifically that the hero will ultimately triumph over "the evil character" whether within ourselves, or the world around us.

The point I am making is that any breakthrough whether it be through technological advancement or medical science, or even the introduction of a new medium such as social networking and all that it entails, is open to the influence of two extremes.

On the one hand, there is the question that asks if the popularity of social media can be practically monetized to the same level that traditional media such as television, print and radio had enjoyed in their past glory days - emphasis on the word *past*.

Of even greater interest is if the new media moguls even know how to weave high transactional activity into gold?

It is an interesting question, especially given a December 2, 2008 article titled "Twitter CEO: The revenue's coming soon, but I won't tell you how."In response to questions surrounding Twitter's ability to produce tangible revenue, CEO Evan Williams "brushed off again criticism that the company is slow to turn on its revenue generating engines."While some felt that Evans "was a bit lost on the revenue front," others got the impression as he spoke further that "he actually had a plan.

The Williams response, which lacks the certainty of a proactive visionary path, is more in line with a group of guys who woke up one morning and found to their surprise that their simple idea had turned into a global phenomenon. To be even more succinct, there wasn't really a business plan or revenue model, because the business almost happened by accident. Based on my July 7th, 2009 PI Window on Business interview with bestselling author Shel Israel regarding his new book "Twitterville: How Businesses Can Thrive in the New Global Neighborhoods," the accident reference isn't far off the mark.

If it is in fact the case that generally speaking social media platforms have evolved to where they are today without a tangible or proven revenue model, what does this mean in terms of ongoing sustainability?

This economic uncertainty opens the door to traditional media industry veterans whose unilateral inclinations towards monetization deepens the conflicted natures of social media purists. In fact for the majority of those who consider themselves part of the social media revolution, the reference to revenue or the need to justify ongoing existence through a tangible revenue model is the antithesis of the very principles upon which "social" networking has been created.

Against this backdrop of opposing ideologies one cannot help but wonder if the debate surrounding the need to meet essential monetary requirements obfuscates the higher calling of societal needs?

It would not be unreasonable to perceive the opposing pressures of society's need for positive and progressive change, and the financial requirements associated with sustaining the very models or platforms through which said changes can be facilitated and accomplished, is tantamount to the irresistible force versus immovable object analogy. Especially if the motivation driving the separate camps of social thinkers and corporate champions is so deeply entrenched. I am not certain that when developing their formula, Richard Beckhard and David Gleicher took into account the co-existence of two strongly held belief systems within one reality.

Adding to both the intrigue and complexity of this internalized tug of war is the fact that even if a revenue model can be developed to assuage the fears and satisfy the competing needs of the two camps, there is still the question regarding the response of an important third stakeholder . . . the user community.

In a September 4th, 2009 article I likened monetizing a social network like Twitter for example, to the Cat Stevens' song Another Saturday Night.

> *"Another fella told me, He had a sister who looked just fine*
> *Instead of bein' my deliverance*
> *She had a strange resemblance*
> *To a cat named Frankenstein."*

In the article I highlighted the fact that "with the issue of identifying sustainable revenue models within the social media world coming into mainstream community consciousness, on-line discussions have a way of cutting through the debate and striking at the heart of the matter."

I then went on to recount an on-line exchange I had on Facebook which was telling in that while there is no doubt that users are making money through social media venues, when presented with the question of what it might be worth in terms of having to pay an access or usage fee the general response was . . . nothing!

Here is the account of the above referenced exchange:

SH: *Susan had an interesting article this morning on Tweeters For Hire! Tell them to call me! LOL*

Social Media News - the Day's End - Susan Boggs - a Global Bridge

Source: www.aglobalbridge.com

Tweeters for Hire! The Associated Press published an interesting story yesterday on how companies are beginning to hire professional tweeters. That's right. Many corporations are starting ...

RG: Those jobs, as they are too good to BE true, most likely are NOT true. I'd be surprised if there are more than a couple dozen people in the whole USA hired specifically to tweet.

MYF: LOL!

Jon W. Hansen: *Here is a link to the September 10th PI Window on Business Broadcast "Can Twitter Make Money and Other Questions Regarding Social Media Revenue Models" that will add an interesting dimension to Susan's post.*

http://www.blogtalkradio.com/Jon-Hansen/2009/09/10/Can-Twitter-Make-Money-and-Other-Questions-Regarding-Social-Media-Revenue-Models

SH: Hey Ron.. I tried to contact you through your Facebook profile earlier but I got some kind of weird error message and couldn't get it. I figured you had deleted me as a friend. I like those odds. I'd love to be one of those 12.

Hey Tina! You go girl. I need to schedule your shows so I can catch a few.

Hey Jon. Can Twitter Make Money? For business owners it is certainly a smart move to make. I've done a few Teleseminars on it.

RG: Delete you as a friend? Are you NUTS?

Twitter hasn't made me a dime. Yet. but my efforts have admittedly not been focused. Yet. I just wanna sell me and my smarts, and not spam to do it.

SH: Did you just call me a Spammer Ron?

RG: Oh, I hadn't even thought about that. Want me to go check and get back to you? LOL

SH: I'll be at @(deleted) waiting for your response. Tweet me!

Jon W. Hansen: It is an interesting paradox in that while the community can make money through or on Twitter, the company itself is struggling in terms of developing a sustainable revenue model.

In December, Twitter CEO Evan Williams took some heat from the media and markets for Twitter's inability to turn on what they referred to as the "revenue generating engines."

The question on everyone's mind is simply this, who is footing the bill.... Read More

On the 10th Shel Israel whose book "Twitterville" is being released this month will join me followed by BTRs Dir. of Programming Philip Recchia to talk about this question as well as others relating to the need for these communities to make money - something that they are not doing at this point.

An interesting question relating to your Teleseminars is this, what would you be willing to pay from the proceeds of your efforts to a social network platform such as Twitter - and would Twitter consider it to be enough?

SH: I don't find it a paradox at all. When you have a free website you're going to have to find a way to generate revenue from it or you won't stay in business. Take for instance Netzero: Defenders of The Free World who is now $14.95 per month. They stopped defending the Free World a long time ago.

Jon W. Hansen: Understood, but the question is this (and of course taking into account that I do not know your specific revenue model), what would you be willing to pay today to use Twitter to generate the income you are at the present time?

SH: At this current moment I'm willing to pay exactly what I'm paying for it...Absolutely Nothing...

Jon W. Hansen: And therein is the paradox, and of course the challenge associated with monetizing social media platforms.

SH: That's Twitter's paradox..Social media platforms such as Facebook and LinkedIn make money hand over fist because people pay for premium features and advertising. Very basic business models really.

Jon W. Hansen: *How do you know that they make money hand over fist? LinkedIn for example certainly has capitalization (which we learned from the dot.com boom-bust is a far cry from tangible assets), but still required VC investment last summer.*

I ask because I have not seen a financial statement for either.

As indicated in the original article, the conversation concluded with my last statement.

Regarding my query of SH, to this point in time I have never received a response to my question *"how do you know that they make money hand over fist?"*

The severy sentiments of affluence is what makes this third variable potentially problematic . . . the belief on the part of the user community that due to membership sizes and popularity every social media platform (or at least the majority), are rolling in dough. For most networks, nothing could be further from the truth as the reality of having bills to pay without a tangible or proven revenue model and resulting cash flow are for some changing the very DNA of their original vision.

This is what ultimately makes the So Act story so interesting.

So Act's founder Greg Halpern's vision was clearly set from the start . . . effect true social change by leveraging the most advanced technological platform in the world to engage, inform and mobilize people to action.

As for the financial model, Greg called on his vast years of social enterprise experience and expertise to structure a publicly traded company that was funded by socially conscientious individuals who could share in the success of the network through the increasing value of So Act stock.

A capitalistic model of conscience if you will, that would serve the dual purpose of demonstrating the stockholder's commitment to a better world while heralding his or her business acumen as an astute investor.

It is without a doubt a program of sheer brilliance in that both internal as well as external stakeholder sensibilities and wants are satisfied through the balanced benefit delivered through social capitalization.

Over the next few chapters we will delve deeper into the core elements of social networking as a means of creating a point of context relative to why So Act may become the model to emulate in the months and even years ahead.

Chapter 2 - A True Platform for Change

"The social network community is on the verge of a monumental shift in which many of the networks that are in existence today will not be around tomorrow.

By evolving beyond their technological origins, the core survivors will avoid the fate of the early lights, who like SixDegrees.com are destined to fade into historic insignificance in much the same manner that CP/M ceded to the DOS platform in the early days of the personal computer."

from the White Paper "The Unsociable Business of Social Networks" by Jon Hansen

F or the uninitiated, the social network concept was originally designed to bring together individuals who shared similar interests and activities starting with the pedestrian Classmates.com in 1995, and the innovative (perhaps ahead of its time) Six Degrees.com in 1997.

While developments ranging from Miller and Buckley's Friend of a Friend "FOAF" standard to Berners-Lee present day semantic-based Web 3.0 as well as the soon to emerge 4.0 platforms are noteworthy, it is ultimately the user experience that will determine which networks will make the generational transition versus those that will fade into footnote obscurity. The question of course is why are these individual links of a much larger chain (re network) so important?

If you have read Malcolm Gladwell's book "The Tipping Point: How Little Things Can Make a Big Difference," you will undoubtedly note his reference to the term the "Law of the Few."

In the Law of the few, Gladwell maintains that "the success of any kind of social epidemic is heavily dependent on the involvement of people with a particular and rare set of social skills." Comprised of what Gladwell referred to as the Connectors, Mavens and Salesmen, these centers of influence or "agents of change" play a critical role in the success or failure of an idea, product or behaviour and yes, even a social network.

The key question of course is who are these Connectors, Mavens and Salesmen as Gladwell calls them, and within which social network do the congregate? It is an important question that immediately made me think of an excerpt from the So Act site.

In explaining the basis for the creation of So Act, Greg Halpern's overview of the network centered on the fact that "Life on Earth in 2009 could be summarized as a series of problems to be solved. The better we solve problems the more success and positive feedback we will experience in our lives. To make the world better and more productive we must all solve problems effectively. This requires creativity at a high level but it also takes a lot of resources."

Halpern concludes by telling us "So Act Network is an outgrowth of the belief that there is a huge social and even bigger professional demand for its platform as one of the key resources to influence positive change because solution makers face big challenges when trying to create major solutions to critical world problems."

Essentially, his vision is based on the fact that "solution makers do not know what they do not know often because it hasn't been figured out yet, but also because everyone does not presently know what everyone else is working on."

In other words Halpern is talking about a siloed approach to problem solving in which there is little collaboration between individual stakeholders or network members. The end result is that this lack of conversational intelligence means that it usually "takes many years to figure out the unknown during "journeys of a global magnitude." In the end, "a lot of mistakes almost always are made along the way in a process that is highly stressful and full of personal and financial failure."

The So Act "Statement of Purpose" recognizes that the development of solutions to address major problems is fraught with challenges of conflicts and barriers to entry. Unfortunately, and for the most part, there are very few resources that help innovators, thought leaders and game changers to tie these complex issues together in a single, easy to access resource.

According to Halpern, So Act fills what it believes is a huge need to shorten the development timeline and streamline the invention creation process by unifying all of the best and most compatible solution elements."

By creating this environment of collaborative interaction stakeholders gain access to critical information in much shorter periods of time. Faster access often results in the avoidance of a costly misstep, or the ability to streamline the evolution of an idea or concept from the proverbial draft board to a tangible production mode.

Tying this back into The Tipping Point reference, how many business champions, or industry thought leaders who are as Gladwell called them the Mavens and Connectors, find a resource such as So Act useful? How many might chose to join a network that leverages technological convenience with sociological sensibilities, while still maintaining a healthy bottom line perspective?

There is an old saying that you are known by the company you keep. If this is indeed true, which I personally believe that it is (although my parallel would be the less sophisticated birds of a feather flock together analogy), the value of the So Act network is in its innovative conversational format. Or to be more precise, the So Act technology is exciting in that it has the ability to stimulate meaningful discussion and even debate between industry trailblazers and thought leaders on the important issues of the day.

Having the ability to leverage this technology to further their own progress on a particular subject, will draw high calibre people to the table or forum. This in turn leads to greater insights and breakthroughs that will attract more people, who will themselves have something to say and share.

It is through this momentum of human excellence that further insights will be gained, leading to an even greater level of member involvement. With greater involvement comes an increase in the collaborative intelligence cycle which has it progressively expands will create enough critical mass to cause the "tipping point" transformation of So Act into a ubiquitous social "change" network.

What Halpern has realized is that the quality of the dialogue between members is indicative of a social network's ability to draw top people to its platform. It is in this area where a network's true value rests as opposed to numbers alone.

If you have Larry King talking about broadcast journalism, or Bill Clinton discussing his pay it forward book, or for that matter Tony Robbins providing a power message, you are likely going to attract a crowd of new members who will want to hear and learn more.

Conversely, the absence of meaningful discussion in a network or its forums are usually a precursor to a rapid decline in the number of active members, regardless of "who" belongs.

With fewer members you have fewer resources from where to present interesting and thought-provoking ideas.

Specifically, this raises the all important question are you listening, and are you being heard within your communities of choice?

In "Amusing Ourselves to Death," Neil Postman referenced the fear expressed by Aldous Huxley in his book Brave New World that "truth would be drowned in a sea of irrelevance."

Given the unfathomable sea of information afforded us through the Internet, this would correctly suggest that engagement, understanding and response is not just a simple matter of getting your name or ideas "out there."Instead, it is the recognized quality of the vehicle upon which you chose to carry your message to an often over stimulated – largely under fed world that will enable you to differentiate both your on-line persona or brand and corresponding message.

Traditional media such as newspapers and radio have learnt this lesson the hard way, or at least are in the process of doing so in what is for many a too little, too late scenario.

From a more grassroots, individual perspective this basic truth was reflected in a comment I received in the on-line Chat Room from one listener during my November 18th interview with Halpern.

This person indicated that despite having 2,000 followers on Twitter, for every 13 to 15 "Tweets" she receives a paltry 2 to 3 responses. While the response levels improved dramatically within her Facebook community where between 80 and 90 percent of all comments posted stimulated member participation, the real story is in the fact that the number of connections on Facebook was a little more than 25 percent of the total number of follows on Twitter.

What this would seem to indicate is that So Act's emphasis on facilitating meaningful involvement within groups of shared interests over sheer membership numbers, is the most effective path to follow if you want to build a real community of purpose.

The findings provided by a March 2008 report prepared for UK-based social network Ecademy provides further verification as to the veracity of this approach through the following conclusion:

"Perhaps not surprisingly, establishing new contacts was considered to be the greatest benefit of social networking. Further than this, a wide range of key business elements were judged to be of benefit. More than half the users felt it increased their knowledge, and they received good advice and recommendations. In addition, support, friendship and business collaboration were valued highly. Nearly a third stated that business networking increased revenue and over a fifth expressed the belief that it reduced costs."

Once again, it is important to emphasize the fact that So Act is not anti-growth in terms of building an active and productive membership base. As Halpern clearly indicated during our interview, he would welcome having a million members by next year. What is different about the network is that the greater emphasis is placed on the words "active" and "productive."

In this way, So Act is more representative of the timeless principles associated with L.J. Hanifan's 1916 definition of social capital which was my lead-in commentary for the June 4th, 2009 PI Window on Business segment "The Psychology of Social Networking."

According to Hanifan, social capital is defined as *". . .that in life which tends to make these tangible substances count for most in the daily lives of people: namely good will, fellowship, sympathy, and social intercourse among the individuals and families who make up a social unit... The individual is helpless socially, if left to himself... If he comes into contact with his neighbor, and they with other neighbors, there will be accumulation of social capital, which may immediately satisfy his social needs and which may bear a social potentiality sufficient to the substantial improvement of living conditions in the whole community. The community as a whole will benefit by the cooperation of all its parts, while the individual will find in his associations the advantages of the help, the sympathy, and the fellowship of his neighbors."*

Contemplating the Hanifan principle in terms of the here and now I added, " A 2006 Forrester Report about social computing used the term "groundswell" to refer to "a spontaneous movement of people using online tools to connect, take charge of their own experience, and get what they need-information, support, ideas, products, and bargaining power from each other.

This of course raises the question, is Hanifan's 1916 definition regarding social networking a reflection of its true intent that is best achieved or realized through a face-to-face interaction, or does our current technology driven mediums, while lacking in the realm of up front and personal contact, deliver greater business and social value to what has become a global community? This is "The Psychology of Social Networking."

At the time the above segment aired on Blog Talk Radio, I wasn't aware that a So Act even existed. As a result, the last question regarding a social network's ability to effect positive social change went largely unanswered.

After having had the opportunity to extensively review and participate within the So Act community, I can say with certainty that based on the principles upon which the foundations of the So Act Network is being built, we now have our answer. The answer of course is a resounding yes!

Chapter 3 - Capitalism and Social Change: Conflicting Ideals or Misaligned Perspectives?

"While the rapidly expanding worldwide communication infrastructure is destined to become a "platform for change", it is far from obvious, what the nature of the change will be. If we listen to cyber-pundits (the so-called digerati) we will learn that in the future things will be really great, really exciting, really cool. We also learn that the Net will be "immensely democratic" and, incidentally, there will be no need for government. These views are dangerously simplistic..."

from "What Kind of Platform for Change: Democracy, Community Work, and the Internet" Seattle Community Network, February 19th, 1997

It is interesting in that the above excerpt from a 1997 assessment of what world-class thought leader and social media strategist David Cushman referred to as "Communities of Purpose," is heavily focused on the altruistic promise that originated with the American and Canadian-based "free-nets" that came into existence during the mid-1980s.

Free-nets according to a Doctoral Thesis by Reinde Rustema titled "The Rise and Fall of DDS (evaluating the ambitions of Amsterdam's Digital City)," are "computer networks that are situated in a specific geographical place, like a town or rural area, on which communication takes place between citizens about their already existing community in real life."

Rustema went on to state that the term free-net was "introduced by the National Public Telecomputing Network in the US for the initiatives in this field," and that the people "operating these networks, for which the generic term 'Community Network' (CN) is used, cooperated worldwide in a Community Network Movement."

According to the paper, and at that time, these "special kind of virtual communities elicited high expectations," in that they were viewed as a means to "empower people to improve their physical communities using this free communication space."

Similar to the differences between the traditional journalists and the citizen journalists whose rise to prominence has been fuelled by the advent of social networking, these communities provided an alternative to the "top down mass-communication media that set the agenda in unsolicited and perhaps harmful ways," proclaimed one of its chief champions Doug Schuler.

In a sort of ironic big brother meets social activist twist, Walt Kelly's 1970 Earth Day poster quote that "We have met the enemy, and he is us," seems appropriate as present day social networks have made each and every one of us journalists and therefore potential agents of change for better or for worse.

While Rustema's thesis can ruminate higher philosophical questions such as "what has become of the community networking ideals of the earlier time," including the intentions associated with the movement's original vision, we are at a much different, and I would suggest better place of understanding today. Especially when we consider his suggested conclusion that "free and open information and communication space can hardly be institutionalized."

Referencing the "success of the Internet" in regard to open standards and protocols which as he put it "respects the gift economy in cyberspace," the framework by which he made his assessment is no longer valid today.

This is due in large part to the fact that at the time the thesis was written regarding the Amsterdam Virtual City (otherwise referred to as De Digitale Stad or DDS), there was a clear difference between Community Networks and the Internet. Specifically, and unlike the Internet, the institutionalized DDS' closed design seemed to be geared more towards becoming a "broadcaster and mass communicator" instead of the hoped for community.

The end result is that users became "passive" customers of a telecommunication service in which the "major achievement of DDS" was that it contributed expanded "computing power, disk space and connectivity to the Internet," in much the same fashion that "academic and research institutes" had done in the early years of the Internet.

With Cushman's Communities of Purpose paradigm, the monetization and control of the infrastructure today is no longer an issue, at least not within the same dynamic framework, as the Internet is the sole facilitator or medium of interaction between individuals.

This of course raises a variety of interesting questions especially as it relates to monetizing the open access through which social networks such as a LinkedIn, Facebook or Twitter are managed by their respective interests. In particular the limitation imposed by some networks as to the total number of contacts one can have within its virtual realm, or the means and frequency through which information can be disseminated has at times stirred the member denizens to cry foul.

This transition from the technically-oriented concerns regarding closed designs that marked the DDS-type era, have apparently ceded to issues associated with electronic freedom of speech and the right to virtually gather peacefully regardless of number.

Exacerbating increasing tension levels within some social networks, and this is an added dimension, is the belief that the motives for said limitations are more deeply rooted in financial considerations and the need for the network to make money versus the result of a deeply held social conviction or the collective best interests of the community as a whole.

In short, what was once completely open and free is now a poor cousin of increased access and advanced services in which limitations are gradually removed based on an increasing payment scale that tends to favor the higher paying members.

Against this backdrop of selective access, is social change possible? Conversely, without the steady and certain inflow of monthly membership revenues, can a network's "owners" be expected to foot the bill indefinitely?

I made reference to this apparent dichotomy of values in an August 28th, 2009 PI Window on Business Blog post titled "The American Football League, American Basketball Association and Blog Talk Radio?"

In that article I wrote, "with all due respect to Marshall McLuhan's "the medium is the message" axiom, while the new media is exciting, it is ultimately as always the caliber of content that creates sustaining value and viability. In this regard, and extending from and beyond the foundational necessity for quality content is of course the ability to generate revenue. However, for the majority of those who consider themselves part of the social media revolution, the reference to revenue or the need to justify ongoing existence through a tangible revenue model is the antithesis of the "social" element of social media.

It is this convergence of free spirited, liberal engagement and traditional, conservative practicality that reminded me of the old American Football League (AFL) and American Basketball Association (ABA)."

I went on to explain the basis for the comparison as follows:

"For those of you who can recall 8-Track Cartridges, the 12 cent bottle of Coca Cola (when the beverage was actually made with real sugar, and was legitimately the real thing), and a hamburger from McDonald's cost 16 cents, you will without a doubt get the connection.

For the ones who consider Star Wars special effects to be somewhat lame by today's standard, and accept the fact that a plastic bottle of Coke costs what used to be the equivalent of three months allowance I will be happy to explain.

The National Football League (NFL) was the longstanding established league similar to traditional media icons such as NBC, CBS etc. To suggest that the NFL had a monopoly in terms of being the only place for an athlete with professional football aspirations to play would be an understatement.

After what to some seemed like an interminable period of unchallenged domination, a group of individuals got together and decided that a new league – the American Football League – was needed if for no other reason than to provide both players and fans with an alternative to a stagnate and overly confident NFL.

It was an interesting experiment in which the likes of the Lamar Hunts and Al Davis' could carve out a new market of opportunity and at the same time snub the very establishment that refused to grant them access to the gridiron business that is professional football.

From the paradoxical differences in branding where the AFL presented itself as the hip, new "outlaw" league which was reflected in policies such as allowing players to wear long-hair and sport beards and mustaches (the NFL required a strict adherence to a clean-cut family image with no facial hair), to the on-field product of passing on every down resulting in high scoring, shoot em out affairs this was indeed the new frontier for a very old game.

Unfortunately, and despite the fact that the AFL was far more entertaining than the run-laden NFL, the reality of finances meant that the league was in a perpetual state of uncertainty.

On the other side of the fence, the NFL was feeling the effects of a make-or-break, Hail Mary upstart that was willing to throw whatever amount of money it had (or didn't have) to lure away top NFL talent. In short, there had to be a meeting of minds.

The rest as they say is history, as the "merger" of the two leagues and their corresponding styles and attitudes nearly 40 years ago has led to a "product" that has a global reach and influence which I can say with some confidence far exceeded the humble expectations of even the eternally optimistic, balloon loving Pete Rozelle."

I concluded the article by suggesting that " the tremendous opportunities and spirit of the social media world and related platforms might ultimately be in a better position to realize their full potential through a similar-type meeting of the minds. At least in terms of the same business principles or mindset that represents the certainty of the established media's ongoing viability."

The cautionary note that I added is that it is important that one does not misinterpret what I am saying, in that "I am not talking about a hat-in-hand, Oliver Twist "please sir, I want more" acquiescence. Right off the bat, and like the NFL, traditional media has itself become somewhat stagnated to the point of dressing-up past hits with what is supposedly a hip, up-to-date look in the hopes of capturing new audiences who now have far more entertainment choices than hours in the day."

What I was talking about is the "necessary blending of the best of both worlds to create a combined offering that delivers insightful, thought-provoking and entertaining programming as part of a sustainable model (re all social media platforms ultimately have to make money)."

And it is this convergence of seemingly conflicting ideals which holds the key to the sustainable economic viability of the "free-nets" Community Network concept. One in which there is a realignment of perspectives in which the best of both the traditional revenue producing business models and, the socially-driven value systems of the emerging and increasingly interconnecting Communities of Purpose are merged into a cohesive track.

As alluded to earlier, this is precisely where the So Act network stirred within me the greatest amount of interest. Starting with the recognition on the part of its founder Halpern that the longstanding cross purposes of capitalism and social change needed to be resolved before true progress toward a mutually beneficial outcome could be realized, So Act seems to have somehow achieved a harmony of purpose.

In fact during one of many interviews and e-mail exchanges with Halpern, he shared with me the opinion of his "biggest shareholder and dear friend" - a statement that in itself reflects the critical realignment that must take place, and to which I had on the previous page referred. As you read on, you will see what I mean.

The shareholder's assessment that the actions to deploy viable social change requires an economic stability, is a concept that has traditionally eluded the siloed mentality of the "either-or" camps on both sides of the ideological fence. A division in which the "tree huggers" fervently believe that capitalist aims somehow cheapen or prostitute social integrity, while the "robber barons" of the corporate world view socially motivated endeavors as being nothing more than sentimental hogwash.

Putting aside name calling and prejudicial monikers, the somewhat balanced perspective of this new breed of socially conscientious capitalist is clearly reflected in the following written statement from the shareholder-friend:

"I find the popular phrase "power to the people" to be quite annoying. To me, unmanaged social networking can be a recipe for disaster."

It's not the idea that offends me, it's the interpretation. We assume that a collective group will always come up with the best idea or solution to a topic. The reality is restricted by the heart of human nature, which is selfishness. You can have a thousand people in a room to discuss one idea, and they'll have a thousand different views of that idea...... most considering their view to be the only one that should be considered. I believe for a social network like So Act to be truly effective as a successful business model, it must be submissive to a purpose or goal. I believe a purpose or goal can be presented by a "corporate" entity, be it a company, government or municipality, political group, or even an individual considered or appointed to oversee. So Actor's can contribute, and no doubt influence, the action or result, but only to a point. The corporate entity should direct the So Act activities to a purpose, with time constraint, financial viability, acceptance, deployment, etc. , providing needed guidelines.

So Act can offer groups for people to sound off on, with no result other than to allow individuals to voice their opinions (which I see as the classic "blog".) Those groups will provide no economic sustainability, and likely no social benefit.

Changing the world for the better requires a focus, and actions to deploy change require economic sustainability. So Act, as the web site is structured, opens up for discussion and planning. Ultimate success, however, comes from "So Do it Now". I believe the corporate support is essential to the "doing."

Corporate entities should be made aware of their need to be So Actors, and the great opportunity it offers them."

The harmonization to which the above paragraphs refer requires a certain deftness of both vision maintenance and tangible/practical, day-to-day front line execution. One that maintains just the right level of tension to keep the ship on course, but not too much so as to result in a break of ideals or values.

Whether or not this balance can in fact be achieved when history indicates that similar endeavours such as the Amsterdam Virtual City or DDS demonstrate that mutual co-existence is tantamount to serving "two masters," remains to be seen.

After all deeply held convictions do not just dissipate overnight. Like the lyrics from the Bob Dylan song "You Gotta Serve Somebody," in which the somewhat "reluctant figurehead of social unrest" proclaims that "Well, it may be the devil or it may be the Lord, But you're gonna have to serve somebody," the prospects for success are daunting to say the least.

In this regard, I think that it is worth noting the final observation from So Act's biggest shareholder.

"I think it would be valuable to make sure the business value receives equal emphasis to the social value. Most of business today is in fact a form of social networking . . . restricted to a society of shared industry professionals. The business value everyone assumes is the advertising of products or services. However, the value of corporate efficiency and expanded development opportunity should not be overlooked. So Act's platform (when fully developed) can empower employees to

increase their productivity, and overcome the "silo" restricted development mentioned earlier in this book. It will be able to do so while still protecting confidentiality, as So Act can be customized to the specific needs of each user."

Considering the above statement, So Act's self-actualization as the true paradigm business model for social networking is ultimately based upon the foundational reality of attaining this "equalized emphasis."

In the next chapter we will examine more closely the equalization attributes of the So Act goals or purpose as a means of both distinguishing and validating the sustainable viability of its business model.

Chapter 4 - Social Change or Social Awareness?

" . . . most natural diamonds are formed at high-pressure, high temperature conditions existing in the viscosity of the earth's mantle . . .diamonds have remarkable optical characteristics."

Source: Wikipedia

I recently came across an article written in May 2009 that caught my attention. Titled "IT Change Management 101: You can't change what you don't know," it made me realize that inertia sometimes has more to do with a lack of awareness than an unwillingness to take action.

While the focus of the text was on keeping resource documentation up to date, and the corresponding challenges associated with an IT department's willingness to accept mediocre results, the premise of an absence of insight or clarity regarding the problem extended beyond the subject matter being discussed. Specifically, the fact that a lack of understanding or awareness represents the first and most significant obstacle to effecting positive change whether it be a localized IT related problem or a broader societal issue.

Even if we have a general awareness of an important issue, how do we know that our understanding and response is proportional to the situation?

Swedish writer and poet Ylva Eggehorn once said that "our position determines what we see."Yet what is our position based upon? How did we arrive at a sufficient level of understanding to truly test the veracity of our perceptions in terms of accuracy and relevance? How do we know that our approach to a particular problem is the right one?

The social media sea is awash with an ever increasing number of networks, forums and blogs. While the advent of citizen journalism has broadened the information dissemination funnel, which in and of itself has many benefits over the artificially narrow and somewhat elitist channels associated with traditional journalism venues, there are nonetheless challenges of the previously referenced Huxley variety.

It is therefore important to achieve a balance between volume and viable discussion or debate to attain the necessary level of clarity to establish an effective and sustainable course of action. In essence, and like the *"high-pressure, high temperature conditions existing in the viscosity of the earth's mantle"* that is necessary to create the optical clarity which is so valued in a diamond, awareness and insight must also be formed through a similar-type process within the mantle "viscosity" of a social network platform.

A centralized exchange in which the gravitational elements of the most advanced technological platform in the world is able to engage, inform and mobilize people to action.

The So Act Network is such an exchange.

As discussed in Chapter 2, So Act founder Greg Halpern's original vision for the network is based on the fact that "solution makers do not know what they do not know often because it hasn't been figured out yet, but also because everyone does not presently know what everyone else is working on."

A perfect example of this absence of awareness can be found in two breaking stories I am covering for the PI Social Media Network regarding important health care issues.

In the December 13th, 2009 PI Window on Business Blog post "Antipsychotic Prescriptions . . . for Children: Is the Medicaid Story Today's Version of Go Ask Alice?" I related the shocking disclosure that "more than 4 percent of patients aged 6 to 17 in Medicaid fee-for-service programs received anti-psychotic drugs, compared with less than 1 percent of privately insured children and adolescents."In fact, children as young as 3 years old are being prescribed these drugs.

"As the single biggest drug expenditure for Medicaid, costing the program $7.9 billion in 2006, the most recent year for which data is available," this is an incredibly disturbing trend which strikes at the very heart of the inequity and effectiveness of health care in the United States.

A point which was painfully driven home in a December 11th, 2009 article "Poor Children Likelier to Get Anti-psychotics," in which one mother related the following story:

"They say it's impossible to stop now, Evelyn Torres, 48, of the Bronx, said of her son's use of antipsychotics since he received a diagnosis of bipolar disorder at age 3.Seven years later, the boy is now also afflicted with weight and heart problems. But Ms. Torres credits Medicaid for making the boy's mental and physical conditions manageable. "They're helping with everything," she said."

There has certainly been diverse and perhaps even ample media coverage. However the correlation of said articles, posts etc. within a central, socially conscientious problem-solving forum in which awareness leads to the level of informed discussion necessary to mobilize and drive positive action is not readily available.

Do not get me wrong, I am not suggesting that there is a lack of networks in which social issues such as these can be presented and discussed. To the contrary, I myself have used the syndication capabilities of a ping.fm to distribute my December 13th article to the broadest number of syndicated subscribers.

However, social issues with the capability of stimulating collaborative action are not the sole or even primary focus of networks such as LinkedIn or Facebook, which rightfully offer a diverse range of groups covering everything from the latest real estate trends to celebrity news.

This level of variety, which is necessary to attract the greatest number of the population, serves as a means of an albeit important, initial engagement versus facilitating a substantive, culminative debate. In other words, unlike the "general interest" social networks, So Act takes the baton of "follow through" to create the necessary pressure points of discussion through its advanced conversational technology.

In the spirit of the old General Electric commercial which proclaims that "we bring good things to life," So Act has been expressly designed to be the interactive repository for what has been referred to as the "series of problems" which need to be solved."The better we solve problems," concluded Halpern, "the more success and positive feedback we will experience in our lives."However, the So Act visionary cautioned, "this not only requires creativity at a high level, but it also takes a lot of resources."The very resources provided by the network that is now attracting industry thought leaders, social activists and as announced on January 4th, 2010 by CNNMoney.com an agreement with Venture Point to "integrate" that organization's Investor Awareness Database into the So Act platform to "support socially conscious investments."

On a personal level, So Act with its rapidly expanding think tank calibre membership, is the reason why I chose to establish the "Pharmaceutical Alerts" Group on the network. My expectation is that the dynamic elements of the So Act platform will stimulate a progressive response that will transition the issue from awareness to discussion and eventually to positive action.

It is of course this third element (positive action) of the " engage, inform, cross-pollinate and mobilize" process that distinguishes So Act from any of the other social networks, thereby warranting the investment of my already limited time resources.

A key point to remember in any social interaction that courageously tackles controversial, even incendiary subject matter is to go in with a position, but not a pre-ordained outcome. While agreement is not necessary (dissenting views are what often creates the aforementioned pressure points that are necessary to shape a collective and collaborative view of a particular issue and possible resolutions), mutual respect between members is essential.

In fact it is the harmonious diversity of member views according to a recent company press release that ultimately "helps you to expand your sphere of influence and crystallize forward thinking into positive action on a larger scale."In short, it is the people who leveraging the So Act advanced technological platform, create the critical mass necessary to create awareness, solve problems and influence the required change (if change is required).

This brings us back full circle to the opening comments from this chapter, in which segmented and perhaps partial awareness converges within a centralized exchange that "is able to (cohesively and collectively) engage, inform and mobilize people" who want to take an active role in the world in which they live.

As a point of reference in terms of providing you with ideas as to how you can utilize So Act to stimulate discussion and action involving the issues that are important to you, here are a few examples around which I have established "Communities of Purpose" or Groups.

Pharmaceutical Alerts Group

Besides serving as a primary vehicle for creating awareness and stimulating debate regarding the issues associated with the prescribing of anti psychotic drugs to children, the Pharmaceutical Alerts Group is proving to be an effective venue for related topics.

One such example is the recent move on the part of the Canadian Government to implement a Bill that might very well sound the proverbial death knell for the Natural Health Products industry.(Note: while the proposed Bill itself is indigenous to Canada, the global implications are clear as it relates to the Natural Health Product industry in other countries such as the United States and the United Kingdom. Industry representatives in these countries are following the events in Canada quite closely as the possibility that they will face similar-type challenges in the future is not beyond the realms of possibility.)

I decided to use the Pharmaceutical Alerts Group as the vehicle through which I made the unusual move of releasing in advance, the questions I will be asking the President of the Natural Health Products Protection Association in an upcoming segment of the PI Window on Business Show. It is important to note that So Act advanced conversational technology enables you to embed links - which I did in this instance, as well as videos etc. within the actual text body of the comment box. This is an important feature as it enables you to simultaneously (and easily) share reference materials with all members of the group.

The following is a copy of what was made available to the members of the group through the link:

Complexity of Issues Regarding the Regulation of the Natural Health Product Industry Likely Tied to Basic Issues

2010 January 4

This Wednesday's segment of the PI Window on Business "Doing What Comes Naturally: Are Natural Health Products Being Held to a Higher Standard," in which I interview NHPPA President Shawn Buckley regarding the controversial Bill C-6 that poses two potential threats to the industry's survival in Canada, promises to be one of the most thought provoking.

As is my usual practice, I spend a good deal of time researching the subject matter being covered to make certain that every show provides listeners with a unique insight into a particular topic or issue. In essence, to present perspectives that create a better level of understanding while still being entertaining in the process. The preparation for this particular segment was no exception.

With health care being one of the primary issues on both public and personal agendas including questions surrounding the prescription of anti psychotic drugs to children between the ages of 3 and 16 through Medicaid in the US, and the introduction of the aforementioned controversial legislation in Canada, I felt that it would be a good idea to make the unusual move of equipping you with the questions I will be asking Mr. Buckley in advance of the actual show.

I am doing this for several reasons, the most important of which is to help to create a point of reference or context by which the bigger picture can become a bit clearer. Especially as it relates to influencing factors such as the economy and the potential impact on health care in general.

Once again, the live broadcast will air on January 6th between 12:30 and 1:30 PM EST on the Blog Talk Radio Network. Simply click on the following link (Doing What Comes Naturally: Are Natural Health Products Being Held to a Higher Standard) to "tune in" directly through your PC.

In the meantime, here is Shawn Buckley's bio, and of course the questions that will be asked:

About Shawn:

Shawn Buckley is lawyer with expertise in the Food and Drugs Act and Regulations. Mr. Buckley acts primarily for manufacturers of Natural Health Products and has an enviable track record in protecting companies charged by Health Canada. Some of the more notable defences have included:

- obtaining the acquittal of TrueHope Nutritional Support following a protracted Health Canada prosecution (click here to see the decision);
- obtaining the acquittal of the Strauss Herb Company from 73 charges brought by Health Canada;
- having charges against the Nutraceutical Company (Biomedica) withdrawn after Constitutional Challenges to the New Drug Regulations and the seizure power under the Food and Drugs Act were filed.

The Questions:

Segment 1 (Creating Context: A Financial Perspective)

Host Comment: In a recent conversation with a representative from the NHPPA, when I had asked for their thoughts as to the reasons for Bill C-6, amongst the variety of responses the one that stood out the most was the suggestion to "follow the money," as it relates to the pharmaceutical industry. Against this comparative backdrop we will attempt to create a point of reference on three key areas starting with financial impact, health care impact and finally the role you envision relative to Natural Health Products both today and in the future. In this first segment we will look at the financial aspects.

As a starting point for our listening audience, the first pharmaceutical company in Canada was established in Toronto in 1879 by E.B. Shuttleworth. In the 1940s, the Canadian pharmaceutical industry underwent a dramatic transformation which saw the transfer of pharmaceutical preparation from the drugstore to the factory where economies of scale could be achieved through sophisticated technological processes. Unable to compete on the scale required by the new technology, small domestic companies fell under foreign control. This leads to a number of interesting questions:

- To begin, and in particular with the reference to the transformation of pharmaceutical preparation from the drugstore to the factory, is this where the proverbial fork in the road began in terms of the utilization of natural health products and pharmaceutical industry products?
- If not, what impact did this "transformation" have on the natural health products industry?
- What, if any influence did and does the prevalence of foreign ownership of pharmaceutical companies have on the Natural Health Product industry? Is it an important factor or element that the Natural Health Product industry is predominantly Canadian-owned and managed?
- Based on a 1995 study, the Canadian Pharmaceutical Market was at the time the ninth largest in the world accounting for 2% of global pharmaceutical sales. According to the current "Invest in Canada" web site, the annual growth rate for the Canadian Pharmaceutical Market is 8%, making Canada the 4th fastest growing market in the world for pharmaceuticals. How does the

corresponding growth of the Natural Health Product industry in Canada compare?

- According to a study from Canada's Research-Based Pharmaceutical Companies, they employ 22,000 Canadians, inject $4.5 billion in the Canadian Economy each year and invest $1 billion in R&D annually. What are the comparable numbers for the Natural Health Products industry?

Host Comment: Referencing the Clark and Fourastie "three-sector hypothesis" of industry (which is now four with the addition of the Quaternary sector), under a "general pattern of development," a wealthy nation must progress through each phase to maintain and/or achieve what Fourastie referred to in 1949 as "the increase in social security, blossoming of education and culture, higher level of qualifications, humanization of work, and avoidance of unemployment."

While the Primary and Secondary sectors, which are now more indigenous to developing national economies, are the extraction of raw materials and manufacturing respectively, it is the development of Tertiary and Quaternary sectors that are most critical to established economies such as Canada and the United States.

The Tertiary sector is services based while the Quaternary sector is generally viewed as the being the engine that drives both innovation and expansion which includes areas such as research & development which can involve the attraction of pharmaceutical and biotechnology investments. In essence it drives the growth of our knowledge-based industries.

- From an economic growth and impact standpoint, where and how does the Natural Health Products industry play a role? Regardless of the degree or extent of the financial/economic impact, is the real issue in terms of your focus the ones centered on the NHPPA's Charter of Health Freedoms? In other words, is it your belief that the

Natural Health Products industry in Canada provides Canadians with the freedom to choose their own course of treatment by offering an alternative that if not available would have a potentially negative effect on health care (re an absolute power corrupts absolutely mindset)?

Segment 2 (Creating Context: A Quality of Care Perspective)

Host Comment: In the same previously referenced discussion with the NHPPA representative, I was provided with the statistic that 245,000 people have died as a result of the legal use of prescription medication. On the other side, this same representative indicated that a Canadian has a better chance of dying from a "shark attack" than they do using natural health products. Based on your research and subsequent findings I would like your thoughts relative to the above figures as well as a number of other questions relating to both the quality and effectiveness of treatment:

- Right off the bat, and based on your understanding, to what are the 245,000 deaths attributable? Is it a matter of statistical pro-ration or is it a sign of increased risk associated with pharmaceutical products?
- What does the corresponding reference to the "safety" of natural health products" reflect? How was the statistical data compiled for natural health products versus those produced by the pharmaceutical industry? By the way, what was your source for the death rate through the use of pharmaceuticals?
- As you are probably already aware, I have been covering the alarming rate by which anti psychotic drugs are being prescribed through Medicaid in the US to children between the ages of 3 and 16. This has raised a few serious questions with regards to physician practice and perhaps even the influence of the pharmaceutical industry. Based on your understanding, what role has questionable

prescribing practices played in the 245,000 deaths – in essence it is not the drugs themselves but the distribution for lack of a better word that has been a contributing factor?

Host Comment: Referencing the Canada Research-Based Pharmaceutical Companies web site, it cites the fact that it's sector creates; 1) a healthier Canadian economy, 2) more investment for Canadian University Research and, 3) enables 100,000 Canadians to go to work each day because of its contributions to health care.

According to 2005 statistics from OECD Health Data, between 1981 and 2001 a drop in death rate (per 100,000 population) for the following illnesses are attributable to pharmaceutical drug treatment; 1) Bronchitis, Asthmas and Emphysema – a 71% drop, 2) HIV/AIDS – a 78% drop, 3) Ischemic Heart Disease – a 64% drop, 4) Chronic Liver Disease – a 43% drop.

- Do you have comparable data for the Natural Health Products industry? If yes, what are the numbers? If no, what do you believe is the best way to refer to natural health product effectiveness?

According to 2005 statistics from OECD Health Data, between 1981 and 2001 the following decrease in hospitalization rates (per 100,000 population) are attributable to pharmaceutical drug treatment of the following illnesses; 1) Ulcers – a drop of 66%, 2) HIV/AIDS – a drop of 67%, 3) Diabetes – a drop of 39%, 4) Respiratory – a drop of 44%, 5) Chronic Disease – a drop of 39%.

- Do you have comparable data for the Natural Health Products industry? If yes, what are the numbers? If no, what do you believe is the best way to refer to natural health product effectiveness in terms of reducing hospitalization rates?

- What do you cite as the top three benefits of treatment by Natural Health Products, and how can you substantiate the results?

Segment 3 (Creating Context: The Future of the Natural Health Product Industry)

Host Comment: There is no doubt that the Pharmaceutical Industry is a behemoth sector with incredible financial resources. This is based on the fact that according to a 1995 study, in the 8 years ending in 1995 profits before taxes, or shareholder equity, was 29.6% for the pharmaceutical market compared to 10.2% for all other Canadian industries.

A December 7th, 2004 article titled "Excess in the pharmaceutical industry," which appeared in the Canadian Medical Journal web site, as well as other articles by Marcia Angell disclosed the following:

"In 2002, as the economic downturn continued, big pharma showed only a slight drop in profits—from 18.5 to 17.0 percent of sales. The most startling fact about 2002 is that the combined profits for the ten drug companies in the Fortune 500 ($35.9 billion) were more than the profits for all the other 490 businesses put together ($33.7 billion).In 2003 profits of the Fortune 500 drug companies dropped to 14.3 percent of sales, still well above the median for all industries of 4.6 percent for that year. When I say this is a profitable industry, I mean really profitable. It is difficult to conceive of how awash in money big pharma is."

Conversely, and according to Angell, "Prescription drug costs are indeed high—and rising fast. Americans now spend a staggering $200 billion a year on prescription drugs, and that figure is growing at a rate of about 12 percent a year (down from a high of 18 percent in 1999)."Angell went on to state that " the prices of the most heavily prescribed drugs are routinely jacked up, sometimes several times a year."

Against this backdrop, there are a number of interesting questions as it relates to the Natural Health Product industry:

- Is a key benefit of the Natural Health Products industry tied to the fact that the sector provides a lower cost alternative to the drugs produced by the pharmaceutical industry? What degree of savings are available to families?
- Many pharmaceutical companies provide "natural health products." Is this tied to the recognition that there is a demand for these kinds of products and, if it does what risk does their entry into the market pose to the indigenous Natural Health Industry?"

Host Comment: In my December 23rd article "Is the framework for an Avro Arrow type demise of the Natural Health Products industry in Canada being laid by Bill C-6?" I made reference to the Discussion Paper from the NHPPA web site regarding Bill C-6.In particular, how the two ways in which the Bill poses a threat to the industry. I am of course talking about either a simple regulatory amendment in which natural health products would be "reclassified" as a consumer product, or the extension of the Bill's power to encompass the drug industry.

While some may argue that under the second scenario, even with the tighter controls, natural health products are being treated the same as pharmaceutical company products, the issue is one of having a sustainable business model within the existing Natural Health Products industry. Specifically, there is a cost associated with increasing regulatory powers that will make it prohibitive for NHPPA members to compete (much like the 1940 trans-formation).If this is indeed the case, there are a number of pressing questions that need to be answered including:

- Are legislators aware of this ultimate impact on the existing Natural Health Products industry? If no, what are you doing, and what more can you do to create the necessary awareness? Do you believe that this is a move by the "powerful" pharmaceutical companies to gain control of an important market, while maintaining an air of innocence as it is the big bad government who is taking the action?(Note: although different, the Avro Arrow comes to mind.)
- Based on what you know today, what is the future of the Natural Health Products industry in Canada? What about other countries such as the US or the UK?"

The key point with the above example is that besides illustrating the level of detail and thought that goes into group discussions on the So Act network, I did not make this available through any other social network group. My basis for this decision is that So Act is a functioning "think tank" that is made accessible to anyone and everyone with a desire to participate in a process that has a clearly defined objective or outcome in mind. Conversely, the majority of social networks do not provide the tools to go beyond the initial posing of a question or posting of an article.

While your submission and related reference materials do not have to be as detailed or as lengthy as the Q&A script for a radio show to stimulate meaningful discussion, the outcome factor was for me an important consideration.

In short, are you interested in talking about it or, doing something about it. With So Act you are ultimately doing something about it!

Here is another example of a group that I have started on So Act.

Will Journalism Survive Group

In July 2008, traditional media industry veteran J. William Grimes predicted that the daily newspaper would no longer exist in the US within five years.

The basis for his prognostication was tied to the unhealthy combination of declining advertising revenues (in the most recent year for which data is available, print newspapers received only 15% of the $67 billion spent on advertising - down 10% from a decade earlier), while holding only 5% of the population in terms of readership numbers.

With stalwart publications such as the New York Times losing money now, Grimes' prediction that ad revenues would drop to 10% within the next two to three years gives further credence to his prediction.

The fact that the FTC held a series of workshops and roundtables in early December 2009 asking the question "How will journalism survive the Internet Age" is merely the exclamation point to print media's dire circumstances.

But as I had reported in my December 20th PI Window on Business blog post "Local Television: A Question of Relevance in a Changing World," traditional media in general is under siege. A condition in which the emergence of social media has played a major role.

Given the changing dynamics, including the advent of citizen journalism, I posted the link to the following television-related article in the Will Journalism Survive Group in So Act to determine how this current situation is actually being perceived by both the reading and viewing public.

Here is the article in its entirety:

Like the once great pitcher whose fastball has lost some of its speed, or the boxer whose timing is a second or two slower than it once was, local television is also out of step with a world that is now dominated by citizen journalism and fast-paced individually driven social media venues.

I am of course old enough to remember a time when only two or three channels were available on your TV dial, and you actually had to get up off the sofa to manually change between stations. Or how "rabbit ears" as they were called had to be masterfully manoeuvred to ensure the best possible reception. More style than science, a good picture and sound was also accomplished with a sharp bang to the side of the set, which interestingly enough seemed to work despite the TV's internal make-up of mostly glass tubes held in place by a few connecting prongs through which the electricity would pulsate. Yes it is true, TV back then was more like a radio with a picture tube.

During this heyday, when Lloyd Robertson was still with CBC and his counterpart Harvey Kirk at the CTV network would battle for ratings (until Robertson made the jump over to the "new" network), locally produced television shows were a big part of a station's line-up.

Delivering a flavour that was uniquely indigenous to the region it served, local programming reflected in a kind of ironic twist, the personality quotient that today's media experts indicate is a key ingredient of successful Internet venues such as blogs or on-line radio shows.

With the world today being a much smaller place, local TV's decline is not so much a reflection of a changing taste or appetite for local fare, so much as it is a by product of our attitude towards traditional media in general.

These sentiments were reflected in a 2009 UK report which highlighted "the fact that consumers continue to tell Ofcom (the Office of Communications) they value a choice of regionally-based television news and relevant local content."However, the report warned "that the UK's local and regional media are facing unprecedented challenges, driven by *growing use of the internet*."

Ofcom's conclusion? An "independent news consortia could be an effective means of achieving this valued choice of news, alongside the BBC, while providing a potential platform for the future development of more local services, including local TV, and using *other media*."The emphasis on the "growing use of the internet," and "other media" is mine.

Closer to home, and in his June 4th, 2009 post titled "Who Cares About Local TV?" Dave Cournoyer added another dimension to this conversation when he openly wondered if he was the "only Edmontonian who believes that our local television stations don't feel very local anymore?"

A fair question considering the fact that following the sale of "Edmonton's two main private television stations" to what he referred to as "the massive CTVGlobeMedia and CanWest Global media corporations," the stations he lamented "adopted the brand of their national owners."Despite retaining many of the same personnel, Cournoyer believes that the re-branded venues have lost the "uniqueness of their former local identity."

Others are less generous or nostalgic in their appraisal of the situation including the Editor of the S.E. Calgary News Markham Hislop whose November 16th, 2009 article headline read "Newspapers and TV Stations Are Sunset Industries. Let 'Em Fail."

A November 13th, 2009 Globe and Mail article asked the question "if a local TV station in a Canadian City goes dark, does anybody notice?" says a great deal in terms of how out of touch traditional TV is with its intended viewers.

An observation that gains further creditability as the same article reported on the brewing battle between Canada's big television networks and their largest cable and satellite carriers over what else . . . money. One can only smile at the fact that these two sides are fighting over territory that is gradually slipping into the hands of the viewers themselves. At least as it relates to local television.

The advent of citizen journalists who communicate through blogs, Internet Radio Networks such as Blog Talk Radio and, Internet TV means that the public is no longer dependent on the artificially narrow distribution media streams as a source for information and entertainment.

It is just a matter of time before you will see hundreds if not thousands of "local" Internet TV Stations pop-up across the country. The technology is certainly there, and the proof in terms of being able to attract viewers has already been demonstrated by shows such as The Young Turks, which has more than 13 million hits per month on YouTube alone.

Some detractors may suggest that sending out a signal and appearing on camera is light years apart from producing and broadcasting a "professionally polished" show. They make a good point to a certain degree. However, TV's early days had moments of spontaneity that were anything but polished and certainly not professional. In Winnipeg for example, it was a common belief if not fact that a local sports announcer may have on more than one occasion been three sheets to the wind during live broadcasts. Rather than offending, it actually added to his homespun charm, which fuelled many a colourful anecdote.

I am not suggesting that imbibing become a part of anyone's pre-show preparation routine. What I am saying is like any new medium there is a "learning curve."However, and unlike mediums such as radio and TV, the learning curve in the virtual world of social media is considerably shorter. This means that before long, the high quality content associated with many blogs and Internet Radio shows will also flow into the realms of Internet TV.

So while the dinosaurs fight over the "hundreds of millions" of dollars that are still available today, the world of social media is forever changing everyone else's world.

Just ask J. William Grimes who at a conference this past summer predicted that daily newspapers in the US will be gone within the next five years. Or perhaps study the results from the FTC's workshops and roundtables from earlier this month which asked the question "How will journalism survive the Internet Age?"

With these market dynamics changing the media landscape so dramatically, local television is at least in its present form, like the pitcher whose fastball has lost its speed, or the boxer whose timing is now slower. Instead of trying to compete when one is no longer capable of being competitive, the best thing to do is to retire and reminisce about the past glory days. Like the old George and Ira Gershwin song from 1937, no one can ever take that away.

As indicated, the above examples provided in this chapter deal with issues in which I have a personal interest.

Whatever your area of interest or passion, if So Act doesn't already have a group addressing the issue, you can set one up both quickly and easily. Once established, you will within a very short time come to realize why this is an "action" network as you will almost immediately be engaged by current members who will make you feel welcome, as well as provide guidance on maximizing you're So Act experience.

As a point of reference, here is just a partial list of the groups that have already been established on So Act:

> Child Advocates Unite
> See Your First Heart Attach Before It Devastates
> You
> Model Your Life

Investing
Pay Me What I Am Worth
Addiction Recovery Solutions
Bipolar Care - Bipolar Advocacy
Anxiety - Panic Attacks - OCD - PTSD and Agoraphobia - The Solution
Food and Drug Regulation Solution
Great Music
Inspire Your World

Chapter 5 - The Company You Keep

"A man is known by the company he keeps."

Aesop's Moral

A famous Aesop's fable "The Donkey and His Purchaser" relates the belief that one is known by the company they keep.

According to the fable, "A man wished to purchase a Donkey, and decided to give the animal a test before buying him. He took the Donkey home and put him in the field with his other Donkeys.

The new Donkey strayed from the others to join the one that was the laziest and the biggest eater of them all.

Seeing this, the man led him back to his owner. When the owner asked how he could have tested the Donkey in such a short time, the man answered, I didn't even need to see how he worked. I knew he would be just like the one he chose to be his friend."

The above fable is quite interesting in that it speaks to several factors that determine the sustainable interaction and subsequent growth in relevancy of any social network. Specifically, is there enough pertinent and productive activity to warrant the investment of a person's time in the community?

This is not a trivial question in that like the individual who was interested in purchasing the donkey, we too "test" the social networks to which we belong to determine if we are going to be an active member or a absent profile.

Like the fable, we are also inclined to make said decisions with regard to personal relevancy very quickly. For example, and referencing Nielson.com stats for February 2009, Twitter was ranked as the fastest growing site in member communities with a growth rate of 1382% followed by Zimbio at 240% and Facebook at 228%.Yet despite this meteoric growth, according to an April 28th, 2009 article by Mashable's Pete Cashmore, 60% of Twitter users "quit within the first month!"

Compared with both Facebook and MySpace continued Cashmore, whose retention rate in their early start-up days was twice that of Twitter's, one cannot help but wonder about long-term trending. Especially in a social media world in which increasing fragmentation through the emergence of new network platforms promises to further splinter the market.

A trend influencer that is likely to become even more disconcerting to Twitter, based on the September 25th article in Mashable by Ben Parr which asks the question "Has Twitter's Growth Peaked?"

The basis for the Parr question is tied to recent statistics which indicate that "Twitter has hit a growth ceiling."This position is reflected in the fact that data shows a definite decline in areas such as market share of US visits to Twitter, as well as US-based search volume.

There are of course other factors that need to be considered beyond the issue of retention, including the impact of what I refer to as the hive and cross-pollination effect.

The hive/cross pollination concept or theory is based on the observation that individuals will likely choose at most one or two primary networks as their preferred platforms. That is, they will spend the majority of their social networking time interacting within these main "hives."

While they may venture out into the vast social media world visiting countless other networks, similar to the honey bee these forays are ultimately geared towards gathering information and insights to bring back to the primary "hives" to share with their established community of contacts. This of course is the cross-pollination aspect of the hive effect.

Given the above analogy, what becomes key to the nature of the individual hive is the make-up of its community as well as its focus.

For example, LinkedIn is commonly recognized as a business network through which its individual members seek to connect to build leads through the various functions of the platform. This is where the technological capabilities or features of the network itself come into play.

While interaction is stimulated through various groups, Q&A functionality and profile development including an ability to request and add referrals, the main focus is on the consummation of a business transaction.

Alternatively, and while possessing many similar traits of a LinkedIn, Facebook (whose core demographics consist mostly of the twenty-something crowd) tends to be more social-entertainment oriented. This is reflected in the network's features such as being able to send hearts and flowers to contacts, or play on-line interactive games. So even though there is a business element to it, in line with its origins, Facebook is a social hub along the lines of an "activities" club. The LinkedIn "business" club equivalent, would be likened to a Chamber of Commerce.

This leads one to ask the question within which category does the subject focus of this book, So Act fall? The simple and immediate answer is that So Act is a unique community unto itself.

As discussed in the earlier chapters, So Act is a community whose purpose is to engage, inform and mobilize its members to take meaningful action on the pressing social issues we face in what has been commonly referred to as the "global" village.

So Act's basic premise of social network interaction is consistent with the universal concept of bringing people together in a virtual realm to exchange ideas or offer expertise on topics of mutual interest. However, it is the social "mandate" or community purpose that drives the unique technological aspects of the platform.

Leveraging the indigenous, purpose-oriented technical innovation, So Act members have the tools to proactively and intelligently reach out and engage each other, as well as a diverse pool of experts and thought leaders.

This ability means that the network is in a constant progression of understanding that paves the way for meaningful breakthroughs. It is of course the promise of achieving these breakthroughs that represent for many, the hope for a better outcome to their illnesses or conflicting social environment, or eroding family relationships.

From a bigger picture perspective, issues such as the economy or greenhouse gas and the Kyoto Protocol, or the proliferation of nuclear arms development in North Korea and Iran are also on the agenda. Think of it has the social network equivalent of where Meet The Press, Larry King and 60-Minutes converge to stimulate and even agitate spirited debate.

The main difference of course is that So Act represents the community's version of journalism, in which one does not have to be a Larry King or a Mike Wallace to be heard. A place of equal footing and opportunity, where thoughts are openly expressed and ideas presented and filtered through the collective and collaborative sensibilities of a group focused on making a difference.

These of course are not the lofty aspirations of a baseless hope. So Act, if not fully developed today in the here and now relative to its greater vision, does have a firm financial base with a clearly defined objective. This means that it is not a matter of if So Act will develop into all it can be, but when. According to the network's Halpern, this is likely going to be sooner than anyone (perhaps even himself) thinks.

So what is the basis for this somewhat unfettered optimism that So Act will perhaps one day ascend the heights of the planet's most influential organizations to become a high stakes player in both influencing and shaping the world in which it exists?

It starts with people.

Chapter 6 - The Company You'll Have

"The world is moved along, not only by the mighty shoves of its heroes, but also by the aggregate of tiny pushes of each honest worker."

Helen Keller

I n this chapter, I will share with you information on just a few of the many individuals and their corresponding groups that have been established within the So Act community. At this early stage in the So Act history these individuals are playing a critical role in creating the network's brand, while simultaneously lighting the way for those who will come later.

It is important to keep in mind that membership in So Act is not an exclusive proposition. Involvement in other networks is essential to creating the diversity of thought and the sustaining energy of experience that is necessary to fuel meaningful progress.

That said the So Act Network is focused on, and is rapidly moving towards becoming the predominant social networking site for individuals and groups looking to drive positive social change in an organized and timely fashion.

What you will likely note from the following examples is that unlike the aforementioned demographics of networks such as LinkedIn and Facebook, So Act's inclusionary focus on issues has enabled it to achieve a "universal" appeal that transcends age, sex and even culture.

Group: Blue Planet Green Living

Group ID: 182
Objective: We are an environmental/humanitarian website that inspires positive action for the planet and its inhabitants.
Management: Julia Wasson (Publisher), Joe Hennager (President)
Resources: N/A
Requirements: Care about the planet and all things that live.
Primary Website:
http://www.blueplanetgreenliving.com
Secondary Websites: N/A
Created On: 11.17.09
Created By: Blue Planet Green Living
Total Members: 31

Subject Matter Example:

BluePlanetGreenLiving: I realize that few of our members on So Act live in Iowa, so you may not be particularly interested in the race for the Iowa Secretary of Agriculture and our support of Francis Thicke for that office. Yet, you may find his observations on biodiversity, biofuels, and erosion of interest, no matter where you live. Francis is an organic dairy farmer whose cows are well loved and graze on open fields near Fairfield, Iowa. He's an accomplished scientist, an award-winning farmer, and a lovely human being. This is the first in a series of conversations with Francis Thicke.

http://www.blueplanetgreenliving.com/2009/11/20/francis-thicke-on-biofuels-biodiversity-and/

About Julia Wasson (Group: Blue Planet Green Living)

Welcome. You're standing in the doorway of our virtual home, Blue Planet Green Living (or BPGL if you wish). Come on in and look around.

This site is brought to you by a couple of marketing specialists who love our planet and its inhabitants. We're on a quest to find organic, green, and natural products as well as services that support a healthy environment. As BPGL grows, we'll be building a road map to guide you through the maze of websites and introduce you to earth-friendly businesses and people that we believe in.

Our focus — where the two of us really shine — is helping what we call ecopreneurs, the folks who launch start-up companies that are focused on helping the planet. We also like to showcase the undiscovered (or little-known) individuals or families who are trying to help in their own unique ways. But, big or small, we'll lend our support to anyone who is working to sustain the earth, keeping it blue and green (and every lovely color in between), just like it's supposed to be.

This site isn't just about ecology; it's also about the economy. As consumers, we can change the world by changing what we buy. And in these challenging times, we all need to be "Earth Wise. Money Smart." It's now or never.

Come visit us often. We'll introduce you to businesses and people we respect. We'll tell you about books that might interest you. We'll review products you might want to try. And we'll alert you of events you might want to attend.

Group: To Vaccinate or not Vaccinate

Group ID: 110
Objective: To have an ongoing debate over vaccinations. Pro and con.
Management: Stella Halpern (Facilitator)
Resources: Points of view from all perspectives. Do you vaccinate your children? Do you continue to get vaccines as an adult? Have you gotten the Swine Flu vaccine?
Requirements: Anyone who is interested in this discussion.
Primary Website: N/A
Secondary Websites: N/A
Created On: 10.16.09
Created By: Stella
Total Members: 20

Subject Matter Example:

Hello everyone! I'm going to start my first message with information from Centers for Disease Control and Prevention, a government organization. Then below that, a link to an article about how health care workers in NY are fighting against a vaccination mandate.

This is from the CDC:

During the week of October 4-10, 2009, influenza activity continued to increase in the United States as reported in Flu View. Flu activity is now widespread in 41 states. Nationwide, visits to doctors for influenza-like-illness continued to increase and are now about equal to or higher than what is seen at the peak of many regular flu seasons. In addition, flu-related hospitalizations and deaths are continuing to go up and are above what is expected for this time of year.

This flu season, scientists expect both 2009 H1N1 flu and seasonal flu to cause more people to get sick than a regular flu season. More hospital stays and deaths may also occur. Vaccines are the most important tool we have for preventing influenza. The first doses of vaccines which protect against 2009 H1N1 influenza (flu) are starting to become available and more doses will be shipped in the upcoming weeks.

How does make you feel? I got a little concerned. Geez, this flu really seems bad, doesn't it? Well, don't get too scared, below is a link to the article about how health care workers are refusing to get the shot. Some are refusing because they don't want to be told by the gov't that they have to, but many others are refusing because they don't believe that the shot is a good thing. It makes me wonder that If health care workers are refusing to get it, and these are the people who believe and trust in traditional medicine, maybe there is much more information we need to have about this vaccine before we can make an informed choice. http://www.NaturalNews.com/027259_health_flu_vaccine_vacci nes.html

What do you think?

About Stella Halpern (Group: To Vaccinate or not Vaccinate)

Life Mission: To reach out to people and help in any way I can. Whether from my own experiences or connecting them to the right people who can help. To do everything I can in this lifetime to heal the planet and all its inhabitants! One of my favorite quotes: Never doubt that a small group of thoughtful, committed citizens can change the world; indeed, it's the only thing that ever has. Margaret Mead.

Key Aspects: Massage therapist by trade. I love to study everything to do with mind, body and spirit health. I love to learn. I am working on writing my first book. I am looking forward to connecting with anyone who shares my passion for healing our planet in order to work together to make the necessary changes so future generations will have a healthy planet.

Member Since: 06.26.09
Joined Groups: 233

Group: 4justicenow

Group ID: 201

Objective: Our mission is to advocate for the humane and compassionate treatment of all incarcerated women everywhere. We work for the release of all women who are unjustly imprisoned, and strive to reduce the over reliance on incarceration.

Management: Mary Ellen DiGiacomo and Gloria Killian

Resources: Both Mary Ellen and Gloria were wrongly convicted. Together they served 22.5 years in prison. Mary Ellen served 5 in Florida and Gloria 17.5 in California. Both women have made it their mission in life to help the women they left behind.

4justicenow is the Fl, NY, NJ chapters of The Action Committee for Women in Prison, a 501(c)3 non profit corporation.

Requirements: We are looking for people who support our cause by signing our petitions and possibly volunteering their services toward our goals. We would also expect people to spread the word and help us get to 10,000 supporters world-

wide. Currently we have 1404 supporters in 25 countries.
Primary Website: http://http:change.org/acwip
**Secondary   Websites: http://acwip.net,
http://blogtalkradio.com/4justicenow
Created On: 11.27.09
Created By: Mary Ellen DiGiacomo
Total Members: 11

Subject Matter Example:

Incarcerated Mothers and their Children: Highlights from the new Federal Report

In August 2008, the Bureau of Justice Statistics released Parents in Prison and their Minor Children, a compendium of the latest data on incarcerated parents and their children. Below are some highlights of the data as they relate to incarcerated mothers and their families.

More mothers in prison than ever before:

- At midyear 2007, approximately 65,600 women in federal and state custody reported being the mothers of 147,400 minor children. (i)
- As the rate of female incarceration has increased the number of children impacted by maternal incarceration has also increased. The number of mothers in prison increased by 122 percent since 1991 while the number of incarcerated fathers increased by 77 percent during the same time period. (ii)

Who cared for the children before the mother's incarceration?

- Prior to incarceration, women were more likely than men to live with their children, be the primary caregiver and to be the head of a single-parent household. In the month prior to arrest or immediately before incarceration, 64.2

percent of mothers lived with their child(ren) compared to 46.5 percent of fathers. (iii)

- Nearly 42 percent of incarcerated mothers reported living in a single-parent household. (iv) Seventy-seven percent of mothers, nearly three times the number of fathers, reported providing most of the daily care for their child(ren). (v)
- Mothers and fathers equally reported being the main source of financial support for their children. (vi)

Who is caring for the children during the mother's incarceration?

- Where a child resides during their parent's incarceration also differs between mothers and fathers. Mothers often identified (42 percent) the child's grandmother as the current caregiver while 88 percent of fathers reported their children living with the child's mother. (vii)
- Eleven percent of mothers reported their children being placed in foster care, compared to only two percent of fathers. (viii)

For more on this topic, see the full report: Parents in Prison and Their Minor Children at: http://www.ojp.usdoj.gov/bjs/pub/pdf/pptmc.pdf

i.   Glaze, Lauren. and Laura M. Maruschak. Parents in Prison and Their Minor Children. Bureau of Justice Statistics Special Report; August 2008 – Page 2.

ii.   Ibid.

iii.   Glaze, Lauren. and Laura M. Maruschak. Parents in Prison and Their Minor Children. Bureau of Justice Statistics Special Report; August 2008 – Page 4-5.

iv.   Glaze, Lauren. and Laura M. Maruschak. Parents in Prison and Their Minor Children. Bureau of Justice Statistics Special Report; August 2008 – Page 4.

    v.   Glaze, Lauren. and Laura M. Maruschak. Parents in Prison and Their Minor Children. Bureau of Justice Statistics Special Report; August 2008 – Page 5.

   vi.   Ibid.

  vii.   Ibid.

 viii.   Ibid.

About Mary Ellen DiGiacomo (Group: 4justicenow)

Life Mission: To help the women I left behind and make a difference in healing the people of this planet.

Key Aspects: Started a non profit to help the women I left behind after being wrongfully convicted. And helping others in creating a healthy planet and those that inhabit it.

Member Since: 11.18.09

Joined Groups: 20

Group: Anxiety - Panic Attacks - OCD - PTSD and Agoraphobia - The Solution

Group ID: 386

Objective: To rid the world of anxiety conditions which affect 1 in 4 people with sometimes dire and destructive consequences.

Management: Charles Linden plus 5 international centers manned by our specialists, counsellors and psychologists.

Resources: The suite of products and programmes plus psychologist led support seen on http://www.stopworry.com/products/

Requirements: N/A

Primary Website: http://www.stopworry.com
Secondary Websites: http://www.panic-anxiety
.com, http://www.thelindenmethod.co.uk
Created On: 12.06.09
Created By: Charles Linden
Total Members: 15

Subject Matter Example:

Conventional panic attack **treatments** such as **drug therapy**, **psychotherapy** and **hypnotherapy** fall short of providing the supportive and informative framework required by sufferers.

A successful panic attack treatment will not only educate, but will provide a structured and curative process, giving constant reassurance and support to the sufferer. **Panic attack treatments** generally make no allowances for ongoing support, hospital-isation will provide the environment required to do so, but it generally approaches the process with **drug therapy** and irregular, short *psychotherapy* sessions. This completely misses the opportunity for an appropriate and successful **panic attack treatment** program to be implemented.

Many **panic attack treatments** concentrate on the so called 'cause' of the initial anxiety. Wrongly, the cause is often identified as the thing which created the initial **high anxiety**, such as bereavement, money worries or divorce for example. These are not the cause of the panic attacks, these are the *catalysts*. The cause of panic attacks is the inappropriately-adjusted **anxiety** level in your subconscious mind.

Any successful **panic attacks treatment** must address the inappropriate *anxiety* level in order to reduce and eliminate the **panic attacks** completely. Psycho-analysing and addressing the 'catalyst' can only serve to focus the sufferer on the very thing from which they should shift their focus. You wouldn't overcome bereavement by talking about the funeral every day would you? It's crazy to suggest that this could help.

Successful **panic attack treatments** must focus on tomorrow, provide a structured, informative and supportive framework and develop the reassurance that sufferers need to make a speedy and lasting recovery.

About Charles Linden (Group: Anxiety - Panic Attacks - OCD - PTSD and Agoraphobia - The Solution)

Life Mission: To rid the world of anxiety conditions including GAD, Panic Attacks, Agoraphobia, OCD and PTSD. See http://www.stopworry.com for global Linden Method websites. See http://www.linden-method.com/affiliates to help us to rid the world of anxiety conditions.

Key Aspects: My current focus is working with psychology research academics at Queen's University in a research consortium including some of the World's most respected minds. Focus - anxiety disorders, Myalgic Encephalomyelities (ME) and Chronic Fatigue Syndrome (CFS)

Member Since: 12.05.09

Joined Groups: 25

Group: Cyberbullying

Group ID: 83
Objective: To stop cyberbullying and to make the internet a safer place where everyone doesn't have an alter ego.
Management: Tess-Director
Resources: Advice for cyberbully victims, how to help someone who is being or was cyberbullied whether you are a parent, friend, or sibling. Advice on how to deal with cyberbullies.
Requirements: Anyone interested in educating parents, teachers or guardians about internet safety, or if you have been a victim of cyberbullying or know someone who was subjected to it.
Primary Website: N/A
Secondary Websites: N/A
Created On: 06.26.09
Created By: TessToeMusic
Total Members: 16

Subject Matter Example*:

"Cyberbullying" is when a child, preteen or teen is tormented, threatened, harassed, humiliated, embarrassed or otherwise targeted by another child, preteen or teen using the Internet, interactive and digital technologies or mobile phones. It has to have a minor on both sides, or at least have been instigated by a minor against another minor. Once adults become involved, it is plain and simple cyber-harassment or cyber stalking. Adult cyber-harassment or cyber stalking is NEVER called cyber-bullying.

It isn't when adult are trying to lure children into offline meetings, that is called sexual exploitation or luring by a sexual predator. But sometimes when a minor starts a cyberbullying campaign it involves sexual predators who are intrigued by the sexual harassment or even ads posted by the cyberbullying offering up the victim for sex.

The methods used are limited only by the child's imagination and access to technology. And the cyberbully one moment may become the victim the next. The kids often change roles, going from victim to bully and back again.

Children have killed each other and committed suicide after having been involved in a cyberbullying incident.

Cyberbullying is usually not a one-time communication, unless it involves a death threat or a credible threat of serious bodily harm. Kids usually know it when they see it, while parents may be more worried about the lewd language used by the kids than the hurtful effect of rude and embarrassing posts.

Cyberbullying may arise to the level of a misdemeanour cyber harassment charge, or if the child is young enough may result in the charge of juvenile delinquency. Most of the time the cyberbullying does not go that far, although parents often try and pursue criminal charges. It typically can result in a child losing their ISP or IM accounts as a terms of service violation. And in some cases, if hacking or password and identity theft is involved, can be a serious criminal matter under state and federal law.

When schools try and get involved by disciplining the student for cyberbullying actions that took place off-campus and outside of school hours, they are often sued for exceeding their authority and violating the student's free speech right. They also, often lose. Schools can be very effective brokers in working with the parents to stop and remedy cyberbullying situations. They can also educate the students on cyber ethics and the law. If schools are creative, they can sometimes avoid the claim that their actions exceeded their legal authority for off-campus cyberbullying actions. We recommend that a provision is added to the school's acceptable use policy reserving the right to discipline the student for actions taken off-campus if they are intended to have an effect on a student or they adversely affect the safety and well-being of student while in school. This makes it a contractual, not a constitutional, issue.

   * **Source: http://www.stopcyberbullying.org/what_is _cyberbullying_exactly.html**

About Tess Halpern (Group: Cyberbullying)

> **Life Mission:** Bringing solution makers and problem solvers together to fix all the world's problems.
> **Key Aspects:** Right now almost done with high school and working on "Truth On Earth" but in the future I want to go to law school and change laws and also open up a vegan line with my sister of makeup, lotion, perfume, hair salon, etc. and help my sister Kiley with her restaurant.
> **Member Since:** 06.26.09
> **Joined Groups:** 106

As indicated at the beginning of this chapter, the above referenced personal - group profiles provide just a sample of the range of topics that are being covered within the So Act community.

I chose these particular individuals and groups because the subject matter they address are both unique and timely in terms of immediate issues. This includes hot topics such as cyberbullying, to wrongful conviction and incarceration to the ongoing controversy surrounding vaccinations.

What was also interesting is that the age range, sex and background of the individuals profiled are equally diverse, from the teen/young adult to the mature woman. This in itself is compelling in that while true social change must accommodate a diversity of interests it must also serve as a facilitating bridge that spans generations and personal differences.

So Act accomplishes the "of the people, by the people, for the people" axiom with apparent ease.

In the next chapter I will examine how So Act can help you with "branding your cause" to gain wider exposure and greater support.

Chapter 7 - Creating An Indelible Imprint

"Branding demands commitment; commitment to continual re-invention; striking chords with people to stir their emotions; and commitment to imagination. It is easy to be cynical about such things, much harder to be successful."

Sir Richard Branson, CEO Virgin

T here is a certain irony in the fact that for many social change purists, especially those who like myself grew up during the "Times They Are A-Changin'" era, the most compelling and meaningful observations seem to come from the corporate realms.

During this period of social awakening, the establishment (of which big business was considered an integral part), came to represent everything that was wrong with the world.

The problem is that this well-intentioned, very misguided elitism created a misalignment between the pursuits of change advocates, and the necessary tools and resources to actually produce the desired results. In other words, there is a symmetry between the corporate world's practical experience of a Richard Branson, and the altruistic goals of an honorable pursuit. Bridging this chasm and reconnecting these interdependent paradoxes is essential to both establishing and building an effective brand.

As I had recounted in Chapter 3, the one thing that initially "stirred within me the greatest amount of interest" in the So Act network, was the "recognition" on the part of its founder Halpern that "the longstanding cross purposes of capitalism and social change needed to be resolved before true progress toward a mutually beneficial outcome could be realized." The fact that So Act seems to have somehow achieved what I referred to as a "harmony of purpose," is a key tenet of creating and building an effective brand. The more effective the brand (in this case the So Act network's), the greater the reach and impact for its members and their particular causes.

The conflicting consequences of this "merger" which was best exemplified in the movie the Big Chill, in which socially active college friends from the turbulent campuses of the 60s come together in later life to discover that they are now the establishment, have in reality morphed into the "some what balanced perspective" of today's "socially conscientious capitalist."

As a brand, this new breed of capitalist still considers the indigenous and long-standing interests of business. However, and in accordance with the Triple Bottom Line "spectrum of values" that measures organizational success in terms of economic, ecological and social impact, theirs is an expanded horizon of responsibilities that extend beyond mere profitability and share value.

It is important to stress that I am not talking about profits and shareholder values with a condescending disdain, as there is nothing inherently wrong with financial success. The differences to which I am referring rest in how that success is achieved, and even more importantly how it is shared to address social issues and conflicts.

Let's look at Sir Richard, and the humanitarian initiatives he has championed in an effort to create a point of reference for the So Act network.

In the late 1990s, Branson teamed-up with musician Peter Gabriel to engage Nelson Mandela regarding the idea of forming a dedicated group of leaders to work towards finding meaningful resolutions to "difficult global conflicts."

While the discussion to realization process took a number of years, it nonetheless manifested itself on July 18th, 2007 when Mandela announced the formation of "The Elders" group in a speech he delivered on his 89th birthday.

Members of this prestigious group includes Desmond Tutu, Graça Machel, Kofi Annan, Ela Bhatt, Gro Harlem Brundtland, Jimmy Carter, Li Zhaoxing, Mary Robinson and Muhammad Yunus.

The Elders, which is independently funded by the group's Founders which include Branson and Gabriel, use their "collective skills to catalyze peaceful resolutions to long-standing conflicts, articulate new approaches to global issues that are causing or may cause immense human suffering, and share wisdom by helping to connect voices all over the world."

In this regard, So Act is its own unique version of the Elders in that it is a vehicle for change that is accessible to all of us. Or, in the spirit of the famous Apple "finally a computer for the rest of us" tagline from when the company launched the Macintosh in 1994, So Act is the vehicle of change for the "the rest of us."

It is in this regard that the emergence of social media, which has levelled the playing field as it relates to anyone and everyone's ability to influence change, is at its most powerful best.

In a recent interview I gave on Anthony Quinones' "Your Point of Q," I had made reference to a statement by PR genius and nationally syndicated radio host Marsha Friedman that we are all celebrities within our sphere of contacts or community. While not intended to fan the social activist embers within us, Friedman's observation is no less a call to action by reminding us of our personal influence in the familiar realms of our own worlds. An influence I might add, that has a compounding effect reminiscent of the six degrees of Kevin Bacon trivia game, or the what if I never existed impact of Jimmy Stewart's George Bailey character in It's a Wonderful Life.

Once again, in its creation, Halpern has established an "Elders-type" platform that in reality has the potential to influence change in ways that even the Branson-Gabriel funded initiative never contemplated.

The questions that obviously comes to mind almost immediately will likely center on the mechanics of turning conceptual promise into tangible progress. The answer is inevitably found both within and external to the network itself.

From an ability to maintain multiple "always-on" conversations with individuals as well as groups that are recorded and saved like an e-mail, to simultaneously sending out press releases on your latest project to top news media and group members, So Act's functionality and real-world interface establishes an important bilateral communication portal.(Note: I want to point out that this book is not a tutorial or a reference manual for learning how to use the functionality within the So Act platform. That said the intuitive interactive videos that are directly available through the site will prove invaluable in terms of assisting you to maximize the expansive functionality of the network.)

In terms of branding, and creating awareness (beyond this book of course), So Act has also established a radio show on the Blog Talk Radio Network.

The show, which is called "So Act: A Better World Radio" premiered on January 3rd, 2009.

Hosted by Marshall Zale, the show's focus is to "explore people and their efforts to build a better planet worth inheriting."

The driving mandate or purpose of the three-times a day, Monday to Friday broadcasts is to "unite solution makers and problem solvers" with the intention of eliminating the "challenges plaguing our world."

Described as a "fellow spiritual traveller and enlightened host," Zale embodies the very nature of a brand that seeks to serve rather than be served.

As the "first social network with a radio show," the Blog Talk Radio venue provides So Act with an ability to extend the support of its members in terms of getting their "products, service, mission and world vision realized."I imagine that it is only a matter of time before the network capitalizes on the emergence of Internet TV.

Beyond the exciting new venues that are available through the social media world, So Act is also aggressively promoting the network by entering into agreements with a growing number of celebrities through the organization's new "Celebrity and Expert Endorsement Program."

The following excerpt from a January 12th, 2010 press release provides an overview of this creative method for creating both awareness and traction:

HOUSTON, Jan. 12, 2010 -- So Act(R) Network, Inc. (OTCBB:SOAN) announced today that it has signed many award winning television and movie stars and assorted experts from ages 10 to 89 to participate in the Company's Celebrity and Expert Endorsement Program.

"This program has been in development for the past month and it will excite the world to know that there are quite a number of famous people with a strong voice for improving our world," said Greg Halpern, So Act President. "Many of the people who signed up for this program have done a lot of good in the world and that embodies our Company's mission to build a better planet."

The celebrities and experts, who were paid with a total of two and a half million shares of Rule 144 stock, will provide a photo, a quote, and their background for use on SoAct.Net and within our network to inspire our members. One of the celebrities, who is well-known for promotion of another Internet public company, has agreed to do a one minute commercial about So Act for use on the Web. As the celebrities approve their quotes and photos the Company will provide separate news releases to let the world know more specifically who they are, what they have to say and why they feel So Act can make a difference.

This group brings to So Act and its membership a great diversity of celebrities young and old involved in Film, Television, Music, Sports, Fitness and Professional areas such as medicine, health, broadcasting, motivation and philanthropy. Each endorsement provides So Act with a two-year agreement that features the celebrity's photo, background and positive quote at SoAct.Net highlighting specific benefits about the emerging network. As an additional element of each endorsement, celebrities in this program will post the So Act logo (linking back to SoAct.Net) from their other social network home pages such as Facebook, MySpace and Twitter, that say things like, 'I love So Act, the Network with a Social Conscience,' The purpose of this is to make the audiences of these popular figures aware of So Act and its goal of improving our world.

Other announcements that are designed to stimulate international interest in So Act, which promises its members a venue through which they can "Fulfill your higher purpose," include the following series of press releases from mid- January 2010:

HOUSTON, Jan. 12, 2010 -- So Act Network, Inc. (OTCBB:SOAN) announced today that it has signed an agreement with entertainment industry legendary promoter Roy Sciacca to assist the Company with marketing and promotion to the music and television entertainment market.

HOUSTON, Jan. 12, 2010 -- So Act Network, Inc. (OTCBB:SOAN) announced today that it has signed an agreement with Creative Licensing Inc. as a "Sponsored By" Status participant for Season One of the Music Reality Television Show "Recreating a Legend."

"This is a mammoth deal for So Act, which will create giant awareness globally for the change agents and thought leaders in our network," said Greg Halpern, So Act President. "Creative Licensing is re-inventing the music reality television show genre in a way that provides much greater opportunity for a much larger audience than other existing formats."

HOUSTON, Jan. 14, 2010 -- So Act Network, Inc. (OTCBB:SOAN) announced today that it has signed highly decorated retired detective and law enforcement expert Dennis Williams to participate with many other public personalities in the Company's Celebrity and Expert Endorsement Program. In particular, Mr. Williams will monitor So Act, and related web activities, to prevent predators, plotters, fraudsters and market manipulators.

Despite its "social issue" orientation, So Act is one of the first networks to go public through a share offering, as well as leverage emerging media such as Blog Talk Radio.

With the recent move to secure paid celebrity endorsements, it is clear that Halpern has achieved the all important brand harmonization that is necessary to create and build upon a uniform image that reflects the true capability of the So Act Network.

Or to put it another way, as a member of So Act, you are not alone!

Chapter 8 - What Are You Waiting For? So Act Already!

"So Act wasn't created to build a better network. It was created to build a better world."

Yours Truly . . . Me

T he above observation regarding the So Act network was of course mine, and it was incorporated into the October 27th, 2009 press release, in which the company made the announcement that I would be writing this book.

I also referred to So Act as being "the 60 Minutes of social networks." This comparison was based on the "probing, assertive, informed and balanced" view it's members seemed to take regarding the important issues of the day - think Mike Wallace.

As it turns out this was and continues to be an important distinction that extends beyond the mere establishment of a brand. In reality, the 60 Minutes analogy or parallel is a reflection of a promise to create and maintain a venue through which members can objectively debate, understand and truthfully reflect on a particular topic. More to the point, So Act is an engagement platform that ultimately serves as a filtering mechanism for the necessary process of testing both the veracity and viability of proposed real-world solutions.

Far too often, discussions and spirited exchanges in the majority of forums in the social networking world are more opinion-driven than being fact-based. It is not my intention to imply that there is no room for opinion when conversing about serious issues of either a domestic or global nature. However, meaningful approaches must ultimately be derived from a process that challenges ideas to the point that a collective and collaborative plan of action is established and acted upon with a high degree of probability for success.

This of course is in line with Rule No. 11 from General Colin Powell's 13 Rules on Leadership:

"Have a vision. Be demanding.

Truly dedicated coaches spend a lot of time watching film, working summer camps, attending clinics, watching college practices, and studying the game in as many ways as possible. They learn what they want the game and, ultimately, their program to look like. Without this type of overall vision, coaches have nothing for which to strive."

What is your vision, or your cause? Where do you want to go, and what changes do you want to effect first in your immediate world and then in the larger world around you.

The value of So Act is that it gives you more than a soap box upon which to present your ideas.

Its advanced conversational platform, which enables you to inject all forms of media into an actual, live discussion stream transcends the written word to encompass both audio and video elements.

Just imagine how much more of an impact your point of view will deliver with powerful images from a video, or actually hearing the cries for help from a region in crisis. As a writer, words have always been my most effective way of com-municating the intensity and atmosphere of a story. So Act quite simply adds another, important dimension that doesn't exist within any other social network.

With the vehicle for sharing ideas and implementing plans of positive action firmly in place, and the rapidly increasing awareness that comes from a truly unique vision that puts you on a world stage, there is only one question left to ask and answer!

What are YOU waiting for? So Act Already!

Appendix A - So Act! Examples of Proactive Response

So Act Network Launches Additional Initiatives to Assist Haiti Earthquake Relief Effort

"Helping Haiti" Groups Now Formed at SoAct.Net in English and in Native Creole Language to Provide 24/7 Always on Communication for 'Friends and Family of Haitian Earthquake Victims' and to Search for Those Still Not Found

HOUSTON, Jan. 15, 2010 -- So Act Network, Inc. (OTCBB:SOAN) has just launched two "Helping Haiti" Groups – one in English and the other in the native Creole language to provide 24/7 always on communication for 'Friends and Family of Haitian Earthquake Victims' and to search for those still not found. Anyone who has information on Haiti Earthquake victims or is searching for possible victims can simply join the "Helping Haiti" Group or its corresponding Creole Group at SoAct.Net and then post such information in the live Conversation message area. Every time someone posts any information in those Groups, the entire membership will receive an instant update with that new information. All members who have joined can talk openly and instantly as if they were all on the same phone call. Every post is a non-static, live, always-on conversation and an unlimited number of people can participate globally.

"The very nature of our Network is structured to respond to these kinds of emergency situations to eliminate breakdowns in communication and in the process alleviate fears and concerns of those with family and friends in the stricken area," said Greg Halpern, So Act President. "The 'Helping Haiti' Groups in Creole and in English seek to provide a central clearing house that helps to provide a place to instantly mobilize and empower people into action at this most difficult time."

Contact Coordinators:

Dennis Williams – "Helping Haiti" Groups Media Coordinator 305-803-9766 Sean McNamara – "Helping Haiti" Groups Earthquake Victim U.S. Coordinator 954-261-5188 Dominique Jean – "Helping Haiti" Groups Haitian Liaison contact through So Act Group – EDEAYITI Charleston Madeleine - "Helping Haiti" Haiti Contact (Currently in Port-Au-Prince) contact through So Act Group -- EDEAYITI

About So Act Network, Inc.

Social Media expert Jon Hansen called So Act "The 60 minutes of Social Networks where you engage, mobilize and empower people into action." Whatever the mission, cause, product, service, program, cure, or solution, So Act can help you expand your sphere of influence and crystallize forward thinking into positive action on a larger scale while harmoniously merging economic and socially conscious goals.

So Act's innovative technologies provide a global social network where its members are able to build Communities of Purpose and accomplish and promote all of their important goals without being subjected to spam or ads, and without having personal information used by marketers. So Act's cutting edge communication platform improves on the social networking theme providing businesses and individuals with project building tools, alerting, and secured network file sharing and previewing in a personalized, private, format that cross-pollinates global interests to connect like-minded individuals while allowing unlimited numbers of members to simultaneously participate in small or large online meetings. So Act has a top 10 results ad-free search engine and its press club allows members to share their important news with their followers, and the media. While membership is free, several features that expand network size and capability are upgradeable for $1, $2 and $5 monthly for those with greater needs. So Act also provides partnership and profit-sharing opportunities for individuals and companies seeking to gain a meaningful foothold in the Social Networking space. For more information, and to join free - visit www.SoAct.Net.

The So Act Network, Inc. logo is available at http://www.globenewswire.com/newsroom/prs/?pkgid=6954 ;

FORWARD-LOOKING STATEMENTS

This press release contains forward-looking statements that involve risks and uncertainties. These statements may include statements regarding stock-based compensation charges and our plans to invest in our core business and make significant capital expenditures. Actual results may differ materially from the results predicted and reported results should not be considered as an indication of future performance. The potential risks and uncertainties that could cause actual results to differ from the results predicted include, among others, unforeseen changes in our hiring patterns and our need to expend capital to accommodate the growth of the business, as well as those risks and uncertainties included under the captions "Risk Factors" and "Management's Discussion and Analysis of Financial Condition and Results of Operations," in our Annual Report on Form 10-K for the year ended December 31, 2008, which is on file with the

SEC and is available on our investor relations website at SoAct.Net and on the SEC website.

Additional information is also set forth in our Quarterly Report on Form 10-Q for the quarter ended September 30, 2009, which is also on file with the SEC. All information provided in this release is as of January 12, 2010 and So Act Network undertakes no duty to update this information.

So Act is a registered trademark of So Act Network, Inc. All other company and product names may be trademarks of the respective companies with which they are associated.

CONTACT: So Act Network, Inc.

Greg Halpern

210-401-7667

Greg@SoAct.Net

DME Capital LLC

Investor Relations Contact:

Steven Marcus

917-648-0663

Appendix B - So Act!
Examples of Proactive
Engagement

So Act Network Announces Law Enforcement Professional for Celebrity and Expert Endorsement Program

Dennis Williams Joins Social Network as 'Internet Cop on the Beat' to Prevent Predators, Plotters, Fraudsters and Market Manipulators

HOUSTON, Jan. 14, 2010 -- So Act Network, Inc. (OTCBB:SOAN) announced today that it has signed highly decorated retired detective and law enforcement expert Dennis Williams to participate with many other public personalities in the Company's Celebrity and Expert Endorsement Program. In particular, Mr. Williams will monitor So Act, and related web activities, to prevent predators, plotters, fraudsters and market manipulators.

"Dennis Williams is a valuable asset to any network where large audiences congregate. Just the other day four teens in New Jersey were caught on Facebook discussing plans to bomb their school," said Greg Halpern, So Act President. "They were caught just because of one caring individual, but had that student not reported the incident, the results could have been disastrous. Many of the major social networks today cannot offer a totally safe environment for its members to co-exist. In fact, predatory and dysfunctional behavior of all types is quite common on these sites. Rather than rely on chance to keep out bad elements, we have engaged Mr. Williams as a preventative measure to oversee the policing, filtering and reporting of activities on our network and wherever web related actions violate the good will of our membership and their goals of building a better world."

"I am very pleased and excited to be a part of So Act and its novel new approach to social networking. I plan on working with So Act and its members to establish a professional and prosperous network," said Dennis Williams. "As So Act's 'Internet Cop on the Beat', I will be monitoring the groups and their goals, as well as the Internet at large, to be sure So Act members can reach their goals without unwanted distractions. My previous law enforcement career and experiences will assist me in preventing unnecessary interference with the important activities and goals of So Act's many thought-leaders and change-agents."

About Dennis Williams

Dennis Williams, a native Floridian, joined the Miami Police Department at the age of 20. He is a highly decorated veteran who served 25 years with integrity and honor. In his career, he spent 13 years as an investigator in such units as Homicide, Robbery, Auto Theft and in a Multi-Agency Money Laundering Task Force in an undercover capacity. In his tenure, he received over 150 commendations and numerous letters from the community. Retired Sgt. Williams also received the Medal of Honor for an armed confrontation in which he was shot at and subsequently apprehended the offender. Williams was also a member of the elite K-9 unit and worked with his award winning partner "Nitro". Sgt. Williams and Nitro, in a four year period, were solely responsible for 25% of all of the felony arrests within the 18 man unit. As a team, they were requested by surrounding police agencies to conduct narcotic searches due to Nitro's outstanding reputation. They were also the subject and focus of a documentary which was released nationally by Blockbuster video detailing the extreme daily activities of a police K-9 team. As a Sergeant, Williams was known for whispering on the police radio while hiding in the bushes watching narcotic activity and sales with his "never stop until we get the bad guy" attitude and was usually known to be the first on the scene and the last to leave. Dennis was not only respected by his peers but also known by the staff members of the M.P.D. as a hard working honest cop. In a recommendation letter, Miami Police Deputy Chief Roy Brown stated "I have the upmost respect, confidence and admiration for his work ethic as well as his attitude and personality." Deputy Chief Brown also stated, "I have known him for more than 20 years to be a hard working officer that is well respected in the law enforcement community as well as the community at large." With his unwavering attitude and direction Dennis Williams completed his 25 years of dedicated service with a full retirement in July of 2007 at 45 years of age. Williams is now overseeing the integrity and professionalism of So Act and its members to discourage manipulators and predators and those out to prey on others through deception for their own benefit. This is just a continuation of his law enforcement career in the private sector in which he will serve with the same honor and integrity.

About So Act Network, Inc.

Social Media expert Jon Hansen called So Act "The 60 minutes of Social Networks where you engage, mobilize and empower people into action." Whatever the mission, cause, product, service, program, cure, or solution, So Act can help you expand your sphere of influence and crystallize forward thinking into positive action on a larger scale while harmoniously merging economic and socially conscious goals.

So Act's innovative technologies provide a global social network where its members are able to build Communities of Purpose and accomplish and promote all of their important goals without being subjected to spam or ads, and without having personal information used by marketers. So Act's cutting edge communication platform improves on the social networking theme providing businesses and individuals with project building tools, alerting, and secured network file sharing and previewing in a personalized, private format that cross-pollinates global interests to connect like-minded individuals while allowing unlimited numbers of members to simultaneously participate in small or large online meetings. So Act has a top 10 results ad-free search engine and its press club allows members to share their important news with their followers, and the media. While membership is free, several features that expand network size and capability are upgradeable for $1, $2 and $5 monthly for those with greater needs. So Act also provides partnership and profit-sharing opportunities for individuals and companies seeking to gain a meaningful foothold in the Social Networking space. For more information, and to join free -- visit www.SoAct.Net.

Appendix C - So Act!
Examples of Proactive
Branding

"Teach Members How to Create Web Pages on So Act using the mighty and all-powerful So Act Media Drive and Rapid HTML Web Page Creation."

Greg Halpern - So Act Media Drive Web Page Creator

T here are so many great new things live now in the network I hardly know where to begin. The operations are getting so hectic and busy (of course in all good ways) that I am going to give you very brief reviews here of the new features.

1. Now when you are in Conversations, notice that every picture and media file has the link and the media itself. You can click either to download it. To drag the media into another conversation, another Media Drive Folder or into the Web Page Creator (HTML Editor) you Drag the Link itself.

2. In addition to Media and YouTube Video links becoming live video and usable multimedia, Blog Talk Radio links now become live Radio. To do this you need the file ending in an .XML

3. When you are in any Conversation, you can click "show participants" just above and to the right to see who else is in a Conversation. Eventually, we plan to add live video conferencing to this feature so everyone will be on video camera.

4. At the top of the Network you will notice a more active window with sayings of famous people mostly who are no longer with us on this planet. Soon, our many celebrities and experts which we announced last week will grace that window 50% of the time with their important views on using So Act to build a better world. The window changes every 20 or so seconds and we plan to add a giant library of these to expand your knowledge and wisdom over time.

5. Now you can do a lot more with the background coloring of your windows which is particularly good for developing a personality to what you see and do on So Act every day as you build your own version of our better world.

   Here is a link made on our new web page creator that I made to show you how I have colorized my So Act Network Screen.

   http://soact.net/index.php?op=serve&file=3733

   There are hundreds of combinations so play around with it.

6. The Media Drive is my pride and joy because you can build web pages in a few minutes and link them to your personal profile and your Groups in just another minute. This is very powerful because those pages are all live on the web and for those that build good pages they eventually will become relevant in Google Searches the way Wikipedia is now. This is like getting a new piece of free real estate on the web.

To get you started, I hope you will immediately join my new Group and follow the simple instructions in the welcome message to get your feet wet. The Group is called - "So Act Media Drive Web Page Creator".

After I get more adept at this powerful new productivity tool, I will share more including an instructional video we will put on our Tutorial Page in the next week or two. I can assure you this - even if you have no experience putting together a web page, this is the easiest web starter out there. It's free and creates instant gratification.

Lastly, in your Media Drive there is a Public Check box next to each web page you develop and all your other files. If you want other people to see those items you check public. If you want certain things to be private, be sure you don't check public and when others look at unchecked files on the web, it will say permission denied.

Too many other things are going on to cover them all so get started on these elements and enjoy your substantial increase in productivity and better networking.

One other thing, we have an English and Creole Group for the Haiti Earthquake victims. In addition to the thousands of casualties, there are probably a few million family and friends around the world who need to find out whether anyone they know is a victim. That is why we set up these Groups. So if you know someone who might be concerned and have a need for this information, get them to post whatever they know or who they are trying to learn about in the Groups to create a conduit for these people. As you know every post goes out to whoever is in a Group so that everyone is always updated in real time.

About the Author

J on William Hansen was born in Winnipeg, Manitoba on July 21, 1959.

Now living in Buckingham, Quebec which is a small town of approximately 12,000 people that is 20 minutes outside of Canada's Capital, Ottawa, Jon and his family Jennifer, Savannah Maria, Pierce Christian and a new addition that is scheduled to appear in July live a peaceful and satisfying life that includes volunteering at the local Legion where Jennifer is President for the Ladies Auxiliary, as well as pursuing both family and individual interests such as art and dance. Since the release of his last book in November 2009, The Hansen's have added to their personal animal preserve of Capone (a Lhasa Apso), Psang Psang (a Shitz Tzu), and Flower (a Hampster), Rosie who is an incredibly beautiful kitten that was born in the wild and was delivered to the family's back porch by its caring mother. All take turns in looking after the mother (Sylvester) as well, through the provision of daily meals and a hastily constructed outdoor abode.

In May 2001 Jon sold his company for $12 million dollars – mostly shares and debentures, only to see the dot com bust erode away his personal wealth to practically nothing by 2007. This as it turns out was the catalyst that caused him to pursue his present endeavour in the world of social media.

Today, the PI Social Media Network is viewed as being one of the top networks in the industry in terms of innovation and quality of content. The flagship Procurement Insights is actually the number one sponsored blog in its industry sector in total number of sponsors, and industry follows rate the PI Window on Business Show as one of the most popular in North America.

Besides writing more than 700 articles and white papers, Jon is also a highly regarded speaker addressing audiences of all sizes ranging from 10 to 20 people in a seminar to giving a keynote address to 400 professionals at major conferences.

This is Jon's second book. The first titled "Your Show Will Go Live in 5 Seconds (Confessions of a Blog Talk Radio Host)" shared his experiences in creating and producing a radio program that enables the reader to leverage the mediums of Internet radio, podcasting and webinars to both establish and strengthen their personal brand.

www.ingramcontent.com/pod-product-compliance
Lightning Source LLC
Chambersburg PA
CBHW051100050326
40690CB00006B/764